Passages

TIMELESS VOYAGES OF SPIRIT

 CHRYSALIS BOOKS / *Swedenborg Foundation Publishers*

Passages

TIMELESS VOYAGES OF SPIRIT

Edited by Carol S. Lawson & Robert F. Lawson

THE CHRYSALIS READER is a book series that examines themes related to the universal quest for wisdom. Inspired by the concepts of Emanuel Swedenborg, each volume presents original short stories, essays, poetry, and art exploring the spiritual dimensions of a chosen theme. Works are selected by the series editors. For information on future themes or submission of original writings, contact Carol S. Lawson, 1745 Gravel Hill Road, Dillwyn, Virginia 23936.

©2006 by the Swedenborg Foundation Publishers

LIBRARY OF CONGRESS CATALOGING-IN-PUBLICATION DATA
Passages: timeless voyages of spirit /
Carol S. Lawson and Robert F. Lawson, editors.
p. cm. — (Chrysalis reader; v. 13)
ISBN-13: 978-0-87785-237-7
1. Conduct of life—Literary collections. 2. American literature—21st century.
I. Lawson, Carol S. II. Lawson, Robert F., 1948– III. Title. IV. Series.
PS536.3.P37 2006
810.8'353—dc22
2006024567

CHRYSALIS BOOKS
Swedenborg Foundation Publishers
320 North Church Street
West Chester, Pennsylvania 19380

Contents

Thomas Eakins.
*John Biglin
in a Single Scull.*
Oil on canvas,
24⅜ x 16 in., 1874.
Yale University Art
Gallery, New Haven,
Connecticut.
Whitney Collections
of Sporting Art, given
in memory of Harry Payne
Whitney, B.A. 1894,
and Payne Whitney,
B.A. 1898, by Francis P.
Garvan, B.A. 1897,
M.A. (Hon.) 1922.

Ghost Ship

SUMMER 1959. Fogged in, our chartered cruising boat approaches with caution Swans Island off the coast of Maine. My cousin and I, young boys, are wearing orange life jackets. Holding on to the head stays, we peer from the bow into the motionless mist, looking for the light from Burnt Coat Harbor lighthouse or for a red or black channel marker. In the dead calm there is no sound in front but the lap of gray-green water as we motor forward. These coastal waters with their granite ledge rock are unforgiving to wooden-hulled craft.

Wickham Skinner. Pulpit Harbor, North Haven Island, Maine. Photograph, 2006.

"Do you see anything?" my uncle calls out over the drone of the engine. "No. Nothing," we shout back. I rub my eyes and look even harder into the fog. I imagine a great three-masted ship appearing across our bow, like the wreck we saw in the mud flats in Wiscasset. My cousin slaps my arm with a piece of seaweed from the anchor chain. I nearly jump out of my skin. "Hey. Cut that out!" I hiss. This is no time for joking around, I think. In the end, through a combination of cool-headed navigating and a little luck, we reach the harbor safely and anchor for the night.

Some passages have a way of sticking with us. Recalling the excitement of finding Swans Island emerges for me years later, intact from the mist of memory. When reconstructing historical events, sometimes a facsimile is all that we have to work with. The cover of this Reader, *Boatdeck, Cunarder* (1923), with funnels and vents of a Cunard ocean liner, is in fact a ghost ship. The original 18x12-foot painting disappeared during WWII. Like the Lost Generation of American expatriates, all that is left of Gerald Murphy's artistic voyage into post-WWI Europe are the stories associated with him and his wife, a limited number of his paintings, and only this photograph of the ocean liner.

No matter which byways we choose, we are all traveling our own paths of adventure. *Passages: Timeless Voyages of Spirit* explores moments when people are fully engaged in, or caught unaware by, the business of living. This collection of essays, poetry, and stories combines the whimsy one finds in fairytales with the realities of life-changing events. Breaking out of predictable routine, the writers discover unexpected vistas of youth, middle age, and beyond. Through imaginative interplay of past and present, coupled with moments of self-awareness, *Passages* leads to watershed events, moments that provide new understandings of who we are as we journey through life.

Being comfortable in our own skins—accepting our paths of discovery as necessarily unique—enables the narrators of these essays, poetry, and stories to travel far and wide. Each writer shows that being who we are while living in the moment is the big ticket—our progress determined as much by our perception of ourselves and our surroundings as by our trajectory through space and time. "In the inner meaning of the Word," Swedenborg wrote, "*to journey* refers to the pattern and sequence of life." To that end, perhaps dawn's breaking light and color is a precursor of separation and growth, preparing us for our voyage out and return, transformed, to the place of beginning.

The Road

One morning, waking, I understand that
much life lies behind me, so far back
on the road that I can no longer see it.

Places don't simply cease to exist
because we've left them. New travelers are
exploring the moments we once inhabited.

I've been wrestling with a dusty angel,
trying to brush his handprints off my shirt
while asking what became of the spring light.

Are the things we surround ourselves with
alive or are they merely mementos?
Are they inert and heavy, or do they fly?

When we first lived together, what awkward
honesty that required of us. Claiming
few things or victories, we were rich in desire.

The road that passes your door has never
stopped waiting for you. Be like the daffodils:
Open beyond yourself to become yourself.

THOMAS R. SMITH is the author of several books of poems, most recently *The Dark Indigo Current* (Holy Cow! Press) and *Winter Hours* (Red Dragonfly Press). He teaches poetry at the Loft Literary Center in Minneapolis and lives on the Kinnickinnic River in River Falls, Wisconsin. He believes in poetry as a way of realizing that other world of "our better angels."

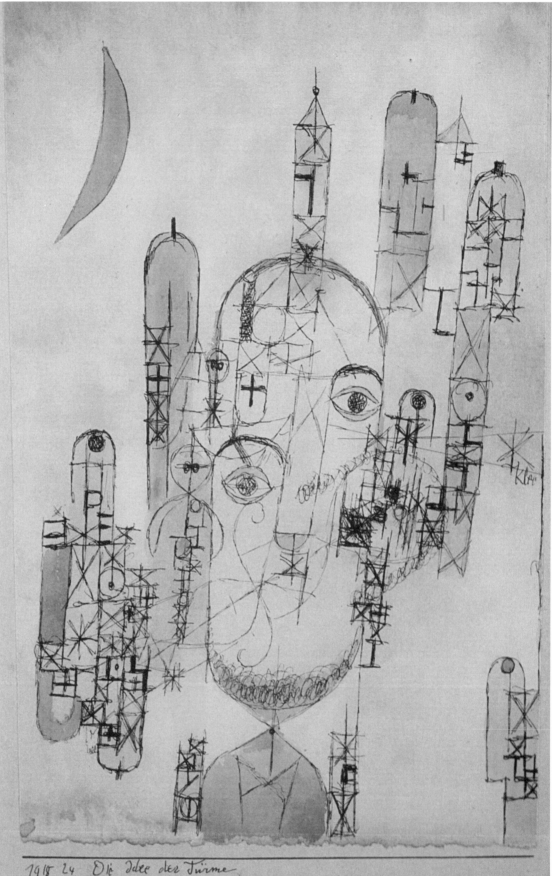

1918 24 Die Idee der Türme

Approaching the Eye of the Needle

THERE WAS A GATE IN OLD JERUSALEM near the South Wall called the "Eye of the Needle." So narrow was this passageway that a camel laden with cargo could not pass through. This left the camel driver with limited options—all of them less than ideal and all of them requiring a man of some particular skill or virtue.

One of the options was to unburden the camel to get it through. This meant minutes or hours of untying straps, loosening ropes, lowering the cargo to the ground, leading the camel through the narrow archway, carrying the cargo through, and then reloading the cargo on the camel's back. Such a tedious and arduous endeavor required someone who was strong, patient, and organized.

Another alternative was to get rid of the some of the cargo, much like a sea captain ordering ballast removed from a ship to keep it from sinking. Enterprising businessmen would often situate themselves near this passageway and haggle away some of the cargo at a fraction of its value. Others made a lively and lucrative business as porters. And then, there were the thieves—mostly poor children or teens—who would snatch a portion of the cargo and run off undetected and usually undeterred into the busy marketplaces beyond the gate. Seldom did the businessmen stationed at this gate lift a finger to help—they wanted the miserly camel drivers to learn that it was better to hire porters or to sell some of their cargo at bargain prices than to lose it altogether. Choosing this option to pass through the gate required an individual who was wise in the ways of the world.

Opposite:
Paul Klee.
The Idea of the Towers.
Pen and ink and watercolor on paper, 8½ x 6 in., 1918. Art Gallery of Ontario, Toronto. Gift of Sam and Ayala Zacks, 1970.

Another option, which was far from ideal, was to try one of the other gates into the walled city. These gates provided their own kind of nuisance for it was at these gates that a toll was charged for entry, and, worse yet, there were Roman soldiers stationed there with the expressed purpose of inspecting cargo for contraband. As the conquering occupiers of Jerusalem at that time, the Romans had little respect for the native people. They searched cargoes with impunity, often taking what they wanted without recompense or reason. Sometimes they charged a higher toll on a whim or, worse yet, confiscated the whole cargo simply by declaring it contraband. The unwise or unfortunate trader or traveller who tried one of these gates could then be detained indefinitely without rhyme or reason. This option was not one that any of them favored, but for those who did, it required cleverness, cunning, and more than a little bit of luck.

The last option, which really was no option at all, was to go back to where one came from. Who, after travelling so far, enduring such an arduous journey and all the hardships it entailed, would get so close, only to turn around and go back?

When a first-century prophet named Jesus ben Joseph preached that it was "easier for a camel to pass through the eye of a needle than for a rich man to enter the kingdom of God," every listener who had been to Jerusalem knew exactly what he was talking about. It was possible for a rich man to gain entrance to the kingdom, though difficult and often fraught with danger. It took a man who was both clever and cunning, prudent and persistent, wise and worldly—a man who knew that the difference between heaven and hell was often just knowing what to hold on to and what to let go.

P.J. RUSCHMANN is a librarian at Davenport University in Grand Rapids, Michigan, who is both humbled and honored to join the ranks of other writer-librarians, such as Jorge Luiz Borges and Philip Larkin.

Passages

TIMELESS VOYAGES OF SPIRIT

PART I

Wish You Were Here

Not until moving to this canyon
had I seen a star shooting out

of a black milky December sky
like a silver arrow,
catching the corner of my eye
as the glass touched my lips.

—CAROL LEM, SHOOTING STAR (p. 153)
See also *Secrets of Heaven* 92, Swedenborg (p. 161).

The Magic Rocking Chair

"IT'S NOT FOR SALE," Ilse told the man who had recently moved into Littletown. He was about fifty, thickset, and wore a rumpled suit. "It's been in my family four generations, and eventually it will go to my daughter."

"Surely you must have a price." Corbin peered inside Ilse's small plain house. She knew he was looking for her rocking chair. "You could use some new furniture," he said bluntly.

Ilse saw her slender profile in a nearby mirror. She remembered when the white braid trailing down her back was a rich brown color. It didn't seem very long ago to her, yet it was.

"I'm going to turn ninety soon," she said. "I have no interest in new furnishings."

"You shouldn't deny yourself the happiness that comes with living well, even at your advanced age," Corbin said. "The money I give you for your rocking chair will let you buy luxurious sofas and chairs with silk upholstery."

Ilse knew that Corbin was the late Kendrick Cally's nephew, his only living relative. He had inherited his uncle's sprawling mansion and great wealth, and his business in a nearby city.

"I have no need of luxury," she replied.

"People say your rocking chair rocks away worries and care." Corbin wrung his hands in frustration. "I have so many worries in my new life. I must have something powerful to soothe them away."

"Surely your affluence can find you many ways to relax," Ilse said.

Sometimes Ilse let people who were enduring terrible hardships sit in her rocking chair so that for a while they could find some peace

Opposite:
Marjanna Blackmer.
Watchers in the Wood.
Pen and ink, 1987.

5

and relief. She was glad they felt better because of it, and they were always very appreciative.

Ilse waited for Corbin to ask to sit in her rocking chair, and she was ready to say no. She hadn't met him before that day, and his bold manner made her feel uneasy.

To her surprise, Corbin did not ask.

"I'll pay you any amount you ask, and even if you don't want part of my fortune, you must know someone who can use it."

"There is no one," Ilse said thinking of her daughter, son-in-law, their grown daughter, her two sons, and felt grateful that none of them had any need of Corbin's money.

"Now go," she said firmly.

"I would take good care of your rocking chair." Beads of sweat formed on Corbin's ruddy face. "I have a special place for it."

So do I, Ilse thought. Without turning around and looking at her rocking chair, she saw the pale gray color of its delicately carved wood. It stood in a corner of her living room facing a small window and the tall trees beyond her tiny yard.

"I won't give up until you sell it to me."

With that, the tousle-haired man strode out to the street.

Ilse looked at her rocking chair and remembered the story her grandmother had told her.

Deneta was a mysterious woman, although not unkind. Still, many of the people where Ilse's great-grandparents lived were afraid of her. For Deneta was extremely tall, wore long black capes, and lived in a cave above the hills. Yet Ilse's great-grandparents had no fear of her, for she gave them potions that cured a variety of sicknesses, including a deep, lingering cough Ilse's great-grandfather had. And on nights Deneta was far away from her cave and needed a place to sleep, Ilse's great-grandparents always gave her hot stew and a comfortable bed.

Then came the night Deneta was walking through the forest and a terrible wind rose up. Knowing a storm would soon come and that she was too great a distance from Ilse's great-grandparents' house to find shelter there, Deneta was left to the mercy of the forest.

"I beg you," Deneta implored the trees. "Let me find sanctuary within the branches before I am drenched with rain, catch a chill, and die."

But all the trees cast deaf ears to Deneta, except for one.

It was smaller than the others. Its bark was torn in many spots up and down the tree's trunk, exposing wood of a whispery shade of gray. Its leafy branches were not nearly as thick and full as the other trees, yet this scrawny tree extended its strongest branch to Deneta. She climbed up, the tree cupped its branches together tightly to protect her, and she stayed warm and dry during the storm. When it was over, the tree loosened its branches, and Deneta slid gently to the ground.

She gazed at the tree that had shielded her.

"Long after your fellow trees turn to dust, may you bring comfort, joy, and peace to all those who sit upon your fine wood."

Then Deneta tapped the scraggly tree with her thumb, creating for an instant a bright aqua light that could be seen for miles around.

One year later a fire swept through the forest. Only the tree that had protected Deneta remained standing. The local people became afraid of that tree because Deneta told them how it had given her refuge during the worst storm the area had known in one-hundred years. So, believing the little tree was bewitched, they said it must be chopped down. They also decided to burn the wood, but when it would not catch fire, Ilse's great-grandfather took the wood home and made a rocking chair from it.

Deneta saw this and rejoiced.

"It will never leave your family," she said to Ilse's great-grandparents. She touched the rocking chair, and for a second it glowed with purple light. "For thousands of years to come, it will give great calmness and happiness to all who rest on it."

Before Ilse went to sit in her unique rocking chair, she watched Corbin turn the corner one block away. She knew he would soon walk past her church, where in one week she would be attending a party honoring her ninetieth birthday.

Don't come back here if you still think you can own my rocking chair, Ilse thought. Many have tried before you, and none have succeeded.

Then she sat in it and spent the next two hours feeling blissful.

The next morning Ilse watched a young man holding a huge bouquet of orange tulips approach her house. Behind him stood a truckload of red, yellow, pink, and orange tulips.

"For you, Miss Ilse," the young man said, handing her the gorgeous flowers. He gestured to the sea of blossoms in his truck that awaited planting in Ilse's garden. "That bouquet and every tulip here are gifts from Corbin Cally. Also from Mr. Cally is myself in service to you as gardener of all these fine flowers."

Ilse recognized the young man. He was the son of the town florist, who knew how much Ilse loved orange tulips.

"Take all of them away, Rowan. Including this bouquet. I have no need of flowers from Mr. Cally."

This, Ilse soon saw, was only the beginning.

Sweet cakes, fresh seafood, and countless other delicacies were brought to her door. Among these treats was the currant bread Ilse was so fond of but could not purchase anywhere in Littletown. With each of these deliveries, Corbin sent a cook and a baker along to prepare meals for Ilse. She declined their services, and all the foods were sent back.

Ilse also refused satin brocade sofas and chairs and gold inlaid mahogany tables delivered to her home.

She sent Corbin a note.

No more gifts.

Yet Ilse realized Corbin had no intention of giving up. She sat in her rocking chair, which quickly soothed her with the great love inherent in its wood.

The next morning a young carpenter, who was also Ilse's neighbor, appeared on her doorstep.

"Mr. Cally is having a house built for you. It's going to look like a small palace. Do you want to come see it?"

Ilse frowned. "No, Gerard. This is just another way he has of getting me to sell my rocking chair to him."

"When people tell him no one outside your family can own it, he laughs," Gerard said.

The next few days passed quietly and pleasantly for Ilse because there were no further gifts from Corbin. With a happy heart, she went to her birthday party. This occurred after Sunday's church service. Everyone in Littletown was there.

Ilse watched Corbin Cally mingle easily with its citizens.

"I'm having a good time," he said. "Are you?"

"Yes, very much," she replied.

Corbin's blue eyes stared into Ilse's brown ones.

"I won't give up on owning your rocking chair."

"Nor will I part with it."

Then Corbin offered Ilse a sum of money that made her old bones shake from top to bottom. Some of the townspeople heard it and gasped.

"I can't imagine such a large amount," Ilse said. "Yet you don't understand, my dear Corbin. I couldn't sell my rocking chair to you if I wanted to. It will always stay in my family."

"I've heard the story about Deneta. What nonsense." Corbin walked into the crowd.

At the party there was cake, and there were songs. Lively chatter, jokes, and laughter filled the room. But after a little while Ilse saw that Corbin was missing from the festivities. And because she had a feeling as to what Corbin's intention was, she quietly headed for the door.

"You're leaving now, Miss Ilse?" Gerard said.

Ilse nodded. "After a little rest at home, I'll be back."

She did not want to say that she felt Corbin had gone over to her house to steal her rocking chair.

"Don't walk home," Gerard said. "I'll drive you."

"You don't have to leave the party, dear. I live only a block away, and it's still daylight."

"Come on, Miss Ilse. You'll be real comfortable in my old car."

"Well, that's very nice of you," Ilse smiled.

A few minutes later they passed Corbin Cally's truck.

"Strange he should park it midway between the church and your house," Gerard said.

Ilse felt her feeling grow into certainty. Surely Corbin was inside her house. Even though it looked no different from the way she left it: windows open, doors closed.

"I'll walk you inside," Gerard said.

Though Ilse felt no fear, she agreed.

When they entered her house, she saw Corbin sleeping soundly in her rocking chair. He, like the others who had tried to steal her magical piece of furniture, had exhausted himself trying to move it. But unlike the others, Corbin in his deep slumber wore the biggest, happiest smile Ilse had ever seen. And for a moment, while looking at his profound joy, Ilse wished she could have sold her wonderful rocking chair to him.

SUSAN L. TAYLOR is a published writer of short stories and poetry. She writes greeting card verse and is interested in history and the visual arts.

Train Delay

The terra cotta tiles on the train station floor
bear shoes, which bear riders, who wait,
who slump together waiting like sheaves of wheat.
With snow, as the train delay mounted,
the passengers dwindled. The janitors swabbed up the salt.
Now finally, segmented, lurching,
the caterpillar rumbles into view,
its perfunctory whistle clearing the rails,
its metal teeth hissing open and shut
to swallow the ridership.
In it they roll back their heads and sleep,
their thoughts flickering on and off
in the flickering light of passing tunnels,
heading toward Harlem, toward hospitals,
toward the trestles of 125th Street and the city beyond.
Snow returns, streaking horizontally in the wind,
nettling the April buds on the maples and oaks.

FRED YANNANTUONO's work has appeared or is forthcoming in *Texas Poetry Review, California Quarterly, Eureka Literary Magazine, Green Mountains Review, Hampden-Sydney Poetry Review, The Massachusetts Review, Meridian Anthology of Contemporary Poetry, New Delta Review, New Orleans Review, New York Quarterly, Owen Wister Review, Plainsongs, Poet Lore, Poetry International, RE:AL, The South Carolina Review, South Dakota Review, Southern Poetry Review, Sulphur River Review,* and *The Worcester Review.* He was nominated for a Pushcart Prize in poetry (2006).

WILLIAM KLOEFKORN

At Home Wherever Home Is

Don Freeman.
Carl Sandburg.
Oil on canvas,
23.8x19.68 in.,
ca. 1940. Collection
of The University of
Arizona Museum of Art,
Tucson. Gift of
C. Leonard Pfeiffer.

This music crept by me upon the waters,
Allaying both their fury, and my passion,
With its sweet air.
—WILLIAM SHAKESPEARE, THE WINTER'S TALE

11

OUR YOUNGER SON WAS IN HIGH SCHOOL when he began his interest in music, determined to master the banjo. He was a bright student, a competent second-baseman, and, at that time, a chef at the Villager Motel in Lincoln, Nebraska.

"I'm going to learn to play the banjo," Robert told me one evening after supper.

I looked up from a stack of freshman essays. A large portion of my past flashed before me, in vignettes. In high school I played the snare drum in a twenty-four-member band. A young lady I was fond of—and who one day would become the proud mother of Robert—played one of the trumpets in the same group. But neither of us progressed beyond "Colonel Bogie" and "The Stars and Stripes Forever." Earlier, we had taken shots at learning to play the piano, she because the house her family had moved into from the country had a piano, and she was the only one who showed any interest in it, I because my Aunt Ruby could play the ivories by ear, according to Mother, and because I resembled my aunt—our eyes, for one thing, were the same shade of green. Mother concluded that I had somehow inherited my aunt's play-by-ear talent. Eloise tossed in the towel early in her career, her instructor insisting that the girl's stubby fingers would never be long enough to reach an octave. My own dalliance with the piano lasted longer, but not by much. I took little interest in practicing, and spending money on a boy who would not do his homework—in spite of his latent genius—did not sit well with the one who had prodded him into such a disagreeable corner in the first place. Mother, therefore, gave me permission to drop piano. Money, she said, doesn't grow on trees.

Our first three children insisted that they wanted to be musicians. The girls, neither of whom had green eyes, chose the piano, while the boy selected the trombone. Their parents, of course, because they were parents, encouraged them. The son blew mightily into a mouthpiece for a week or so before he disassembled and encased his instrument for a final time. The girls, though they persisted long enough to master several elementary etudes, decided that the world needed listeners no less than performers, and tearfully—because their parents insisted—informed their teacher themselves that they were quitting, a trauma that even today disturbs the family psyche.

Samuel Clemens declared in his autobiography that banging your head against a brick wall indefinitely is a sign of cranial retardation—or words to that effect. To illustrate his point, he discussed several projects he had sunk money into in an effort to become a millionaire. One of these was a transatlantic cable, an adventure that excited Mr. Clemens and no doubt all of those who, like him, had invested in it, and substantially. Unfortunately, his cable did not work out, while another company's succeeded, and Twain was left nursing his financial wounds. But he did not despair. He would become an overnight millionaire or know the reason why. So he invested a considerable amount—some fifty thousand dollars—in a linotype machine that was about to be invented, one that would turn the printing world on its ear. Again, though, a competitor beat Twain's inventor to the punch. And again, Mr. Clemens was left to lick his wounds.

By that time he had learned his lesson. Twice he had banged his head, hard, against a brick wall, and twice it had repelled him. He was a determined man, at times a stubborn man, but he was not a fool—or, if he was, he was God's fool, and God, therefore, must share—divinely, of course—the blame.

These investments had cost Mr. Clemens a great deal of money, but he felt that the experience had made him much wiser. So when a man knocked on his door and tried to sell him some stock in a company that the man said would make a product that would surely be the wave of the future, Sam Clemens girded his loins and stood his ground and kept his wallet in his pocket and turned the man away—but not before he had heard the name of the inventor of the product he so adamantly refused to endorse. It was Alexander Graham Bell.

The question, then, is not whether you should bang your head against a brick wall but, rather, when should you stop the banging?

Robert had not said, *May I attempt to learn to play the banjo?* No, he had said, *I'm going to learn to play the banjo.* There was a certainty not only in the statement, but in his tone of voice. It left me little chance to decide whether I wanted to be included in another effort to break through the brick wall. Already the die had been cast.

"In that case," I said, "you will need to buy yourself a banjo." I knew nothing whatsoever about banjos, but I had not been the snare drummer in a band of twenty-four members for nothing. That is, I knew that your skills or talents could be severely impaired if you were playing a second- or third-rate instrument. I conveyed this insight to my son.

"I know," he said. "That's why I'm going to buy a good one, a Fender Leo, when I get enough money. Right now I have one that'll do to learn on. It's out in the car. I'll go get it."

I was taken aback. Already he had bought a banjo?

He returned in a flash. The banjo was a hybrid of reddish wood and plastic. He strummed it a couple of times, then handed it to me. It was surprisingly heavy—certainly enough heft to convince me that it was all right to learn on. I turned it this way and that, and ran a thumb across its strings, as if to suggest that I knew more about banjoes than in fact I did.

"Well," I said, "it looks all right to me. Now," I said, "you're going to need a teacher."

"I have one. Karen Johnson. I'll be taking two lessons a week."

I didn't ask him how much the lessons would cost, hadn't even thought to ask him the price of the banjo. His job as chef at the Villager paid well, and Robert knew how to handle his paychecks.

"She plays guitar more than banjo," Robert said. "But she can teach me some of the fundamentals."

"Fine," I said. Robert went upstairs to his bedroom, and I returned to my stack of freshman essays, thinking, *Can it be possible? A musician in the house of Kloefkorn?*

Although Robert's parents and his siblings had all tried and failed to master a musical instrument—had banged their heads against that particular wall—I nevertheless felt that this time someone in the family might succeed. I remembered Sam Clemens' tale about his failed investments, recalling that the point of his story is that he stopped trying too soon. Who knows? I thought. Young Robert might be offering our family what Alexander Graham Bell tried to give Sam Clemens—a real chance to succeed.

Fortunately, it worked out that way.

WHEN ROBERT WAS VERY YOUNG, three or four, he would ask me to read him something, almost anything, before taking him to bed. At first I saw it as a simple tactic for delaying sleep, which perhaps it was, but the delay never lasted very long. After only a few minutes I could feel his little body relaxing, and often he would be asleep before I could finish whatever I was reading.

I would read him poems, mostly, nursery rhymes that both he and I enjoyed. One late evening, reading through a new collection of these rhymes, I came upon a brief little poem that neither of us had heard before. It was called *The Little Elf Man.*

I met a little elf man once,
Down where the lilies blow.
I asked him why he was so small,
And why he did not grow.
He slightly smiled, and with an eye
He looked me through and through.
"I'm quite as big for me," said he,
"As you are big for you."

He asked me to read it again, and I did. Then he looked up at me and said, "Grow."

"I *am* growing," I said. I slapped my stomach to prove it.

"No," he said. *"Grow."*

It took me a few seconds to catch his drift: He wanted me to say a word that rhymes with *grow*. When finally I said *snow*, he laughed and shook his head approvingly.

This was our first venture into the realm of give-and-take rhyme, into a kingdom of sound that pleases the ear. If *grow* and *snow* fit pleasantly together, then why not *cat* and *bat? Dog* and *frog? Head* and *bed?* Over many nights we played the game. Always we started it after I had read *The Little Elf Man.* Always the game gave Robert immense delight. To heighten this delight, or to prepare for it, I'd read the poem metrically, exaggerating the iambs as I moved along, sometimes putting a melody to the tetrameter and trimeter lines.

It is possible, of course, to experience too much of a good thing. I became downright tired of *The Little Elf Man,* so weary that I wanted to tell its author, Anonymous, what I was feeling. But I didn't because I couldn't; although the author appeared in any number of books, he was nowhere to be found. Robert meanwhile did not share my animosity. His respect for Anonymous never waned. I would read the poem, and like clockwork the rhyming would begin—words with single syllables, then words with double syllables, or two short words, as we extended the pleasure. What rhymes with kitten? Mitten. Bad man? Sad man. We were improvising poetry on its most fundamental level. Bad man, sad man, where is your mitten? Bad man, sad man, it's only a kitten!

Then one evening the routine very suddenly changed. I read *The Little Elf Man,* of course, but I had barely finished when Robert jumped from my lap and disappeared into the dining room, where the family desk—a large oak desk with a roll-down top—was located. Through the archway that separated the dining from the living room I watched him pull out the chair from beneath the desk and climb onto it. I could not see clearly what he was doing because the side of the desk hid his arms and hands. But I could tell that they were busy at a project that maybe eventually I'd have the privilege of looking at.

After several minutes he returned, carrying a white sheet of paper on which—using only crayons—he had created a drawing, a surrealistic work that I had trouble making sense of.

"Look," he said, handing me the drawing.

"Book," I said proudly.

"No," he said. "Look!"

I examined the drawing from all possible angles. The colors were primary, and thus very striking.

"It's pretty," I said. "I like it. All of these green lines going up and down—they're beautiful. Green is my favorite color."

"They're lilies," Robert said. "The lines are lilies." He seemed proud that his drawing was getting some attention, and he did not seem to mind that I did not, at first glance, understand his work.

I held the drawing at arm's length to give me a different perspective. "Yes," I said, "I can see now that the green lines are lilies."

There were some purple lines, too, shorter lines with a circle the size of a quarter atop one of them. The circle was an unbroken mass of purple.

"That's the little elf man," Robert said. He seemed to know precisely where I was looking.

"Yes. The little elf man. And this other color, the red—what is it?"

I knew what it was, or thought I did; it was the "I" in the poem, the narrator. Robert had used a brilliant red to depict this character, a red as brilliant as that on the local fire truck. But while the short, straight lines of the other figure suggested a stick man, the large, uneven lines of this figure, the narrator, suggested something impressively powerful.

"That's me," Robert said, seeming a trifle miffed that I had not recognized him.

"Of course," I said. "Well, it's a fine drawing. We can put a frame around it and hang it on the wall."

"No," said the artist. "I'm taking it to bed with me."

And so he did, and when he brought it downstairs the following morning, the wrinkles it had accumulated while sleeping with its creator gave it a texture that enhanced its surrealistic overtones. Robert, for a time, did not appreciate the enhancement, but after I smoothed the drawing somewhat with his mother's iron and took it to the garage and built a frame for it, one whose corners might have fit more snugly had I owned a miter box, he was more than pleased. We hung it on the wall at the head of his bed. And perhaps for the benefit of those not familiar with contemporary art—that is, for those who lack the knowledge and the imagination to appreciate anything beyond the purely representational—he titled it *The Little Elf Man.*

TIME. A SMALL SLICE OF IT—FIFTEEN YEARS—had passed when one morning, rummaging in the basement for a work I'd never find, I ran across the book of poems that Robert and I had spent so many evenings with. On several occasions over the years I had thought of the book, of *The Little Elf Man* in particular, and certainly I did not need the book to be able to recall the poem. It had a permanent place in my limited trove of memorizations.

I put the book on my desk, and that evening, after supper, I showed it to Robert.

"Remember this?"

He looked at the cover, front and back, then said no, he didn't. "Turn to page seventeen."

He found the page, and I gave him some time to scan the poem before I asked, "Remember that one?"

Before he could respond, I recited the poem, slowly, as Robert followed it on the page. When I had finished, he smiled.

"I remember," he said. "Didn't we read that poem sometimes before I went to bed?"

"Many times," I said. "It was your favorite."

He was reading the poem, taking it in again, this time at his own pace. When he looked up I said, "Well, what do you think of the poem now? Is it as good as you thought when you were not yet majoring in engineering?"

"I like it," he said. "Nice cadence. Easy rhyme."

"Anything else? If you were in class, and the professor asked you to discuss what you thought was the strongest element in the poem, what would it be?"

Robert and two of his buddies had enrolled that fall at the University of Nebraska, all of them declaring majors in engineering, a field that did not require courses in which one looked closely—or at all—at poetry. But Robert, who was learning to play the banjo, had a lot of poetry in him.

"Well," he said, "the last two lines are pretty good." I recited the lines: *I'm quite as big for me, said he, / As you are big for you.*

"So you think those lines are pretty good," I said. "Why?"

"Because they make me think."

"What about?"

"About size," Robert said. "About different sizes. Reminds me that not all of us need to be the same size." And I remembered watching *Hamlet* being performed by a troupe from Japan, how Hamlet at the opening was sitting cross-legged at the center of the stage and how, when he came to his feet, the audience laughed—not because something amusing had been said, but because Hamlet's shortness undercut the audience's expectations: Can Hamlet be a tragic figure when he stands barely five feet tall?

We moved then from size to color: Must a person be this or that color in order to be a complete human being? Religious beliefs? Do differences include one sect at the expense of another? Social positions? Political stances? And so on.

Later, remembering our conversation, I concluded that Robert's reactions to *The Little Elf Man* reflected a perfectly natural sequence. As infants, we respond first to sound, perhaps because we spend the first nine months of our lives so close to our mothers' heartbeats. One of the first sounds we hear after arriving is that of our own voices; another is the voice of someone else making sounds we'll need to hear a lot more of before we understand them. It seems reasonable to assume that in our subconscious we retain the sound of our mothers' heartbeats and, since we now have fully-developed heartbeats of our own, we are inclined to respond favorably to a regular beat, and if the beat is accompanied by a variety of intonations and repetitions, so much the better. For a while, we respond less to what is being said than to how the sounds themselves are formed. *Jabberwocky,* Lewis Carroll called it; it appeals chiefly to the ear and can be soothing or threatening, depending upon how it is delivered. Robert and I, during those early years, had done some improvising of our own: *Now no new nard need noddle over nat, for frolic lies the fanfare in the fat.* The ear of the child might find such a statement delightful; the alliterations tickle his fancy, and the child smiles or chuckles as he asks you to say it again, then again, until he too knows it by heart.

Children who like to jump a rope know how important the beat is. It can be slow or fast, low gear or high gear, or some speed in between. Or it can move from sugar to hot pepper, as long as the movement is steady. To accompany the beat of the rope, they chant poems to pleasure the ear.

Fudge, fudge, fetch the judge.
Mama just had a new-born baby.
It isn't a girl, it isn't a boy—
It's just a plain old baby.

The children do not wonder how or why fudge might be related to the judge; the answer, very simply, is that fudge rhymes with judge. Nor do they question the matter of preceding baby with newborn. Ever hear of an *old*-born baby? The rope jumpers need a line that complements the beat of the rope as it nibbles at the frontyard crabgrass, and newborn does quite nicely. And do they wonder about the baby's being neither female nor male, but "just a plain old baby"? Not a bit. They are not training to be pediatricians or psychiatrists; they are jumping rope, ears attuned to the sounds of words and the *slapslapslap* of rope against crabgrass, feet and legs working to jump high enough, and at the precise moment, to avoid the snarl that might cause them to lose the game.

Nor do the children treat the newborn baby gently after it has arrived:

Wrap it up in tissue paper,
Put it on the elevator.
How—many—floors—does—it—go—up?

The newborn is less a human than an unfeeling object, an "it," and what the adult might call *baby abuse,* the child might see as amusement, not to mention the aural pleasure derived from the near rhyme of *tissue paper* and *elevator*. The final line invites the rope-jumper to count the number of floors—that is, the number of times the jumper can clear the rope without missing. If those holding the ends of the rope increase its speed, moving it all the way into hot pepper, the sound of the counting as the rope hits the ground provides a rhythm that makes the jumping both a challenge and a dance.

There comes a time, of course, when image takes its place alongside sound, as it did when Robert translated *The Little Elf Man* by way of a crayon drawing. The eye does not replace the ear; it joins the ear, and together they respond to whatever sounds and images the poem conveys. When the child hears the line, *A rubber baby bumper bumped a baby boy,* he probably chuckles at the alliteration. When he is older, hearing the same line, he might ask, "Was the baby hurt?" His ear has heard the alliteration, but his eye sees the collision of bumper and boy, and he wants to know the extent of the victim's injuries.

And there comes a time—time being both thief and teacher—when the reader not only hears the sounds and sees the images, but also thinks about what they suggest.

One possibility is that they suggest nothing beyond sound and image. Another is that they provoke a pleasantly wide range of possibilities or meanings or insights or whatever it is one chooses to call the reactions that the words have inspired. Robert Frost called it wisdom: The poem begins in delight, he wrote, and ends in wisdom. Another dead poet said that the good poem teases the reader into thought. Another, using the word *thought* in a different context, wrote that a poem is "what oft is thought, but ne'er so well expressed." When the little elf man says, "I'm quite as big for me . . . as you are big for you," the careful reader finds himself wondering about his relationship to others—their relative sizes, beliefs, colors, opinions, and so on—until it is possible that the reader, having laid the poem aside, can take up his banjo or pen and go about his business both entertained and informed.

I NEVER HEARD ANY MADDENING SCREECHES from the strings of my young son's banjo—not even during his first few weeks of practice, or that evening when, having told me he was going to learn to play, he went upstairs, and I returned to my stack of essays. I could hear an occasional plucking of strings, but nothing to fray even the most sensitive nerve. Without much searching, he seemed to have found what the other members of his tin-ear family had been looking for.

There are times when the sounds of an instrument—banjo, guitar, mandolin, fiddle, harmonica—are so crisp or enlivening or soothing that you are tempted to believe that in the beginning was not the word, but the music, and the music was without words. One such time is late evening, dusk, that period between dark and not dark, when there is nothing in the air but stillness, except for the small sound of water trilling if you are sitting at a campfire on the bank of a river, or perhaps the air is carrying the aroma of new-mown grass if you are sitting on the front porch with someone who, like yourself, is "going nowhere in the fullness of time," as N. Scott Momaday phrases it in one of his poems. You sit looking to the west, where darkness slipping in from the east will soon prevail, and you believe you hear, in the distance, a familiar tune—*Peaceful Easy Feeling,* maybe, or is it *Blackberry Blossom?*—and you ask the one at your left whether she hears it, too, and when she nods you listen more intently, and sure enough the tune becomes more and more distinct, and it is *Blackberry Blossom,* no doubt about it, so you settle back and close your eyes, knowing that the tune will become more and more crisp as it approaches, as its notes leap from the strings of the banjo to give the stillness a cadence it must have thought itself incapable of, until, when you open your eyes, there he is, the musician you thought you'd never live to see—there he is, having walked into your ken all the way from the backyard. Yes, there he is, playing a Fender Leo, a beauty if I've ever seen one, the silver on its neck and body catching and reflecting the last of the waning light. And almost before the tune has ended he will be off to Arizona where he will meet the woman whose eyes he can't resist and,

> don't breathe a word of this to anyone,
> but the catch is this:
> the melodies of earth
> are never done: bullfrog,
> thunderbird, a west wind
> soughing through the saguaro—
> and the fish I'll hook,
> but not possess,
> its body, sleek as love,
> this night forever at home
> wherever home is.

WILLIAM KLOEFKORN's most recent books are a memoir, *At Home on This Moveable Earth* (University of Nebraska Press) and a collection of poetry—with reproductions of paintings by Carlos Frey—*Still Life Moving* (Wayne State Press in Nebraska). He is published widely in journals and periodicals, among them *Prairie Schooner, Harper's, Puerto del Sol, Georgia Review, Iowa Review,* and the *Virginia Quarterly Review.* A book of poems, *Out of Attica,* is forthcoming from White Pine Press in New York. He lives in Lincoln, Nebraska.

A Life of Biblical Proportion

I am happier this morning thinking
that a reason for my many disappointments
is not so much a lack of productivity

as my need for a much longer life,
thirty or forty years of childhood,
followed by as many as a teen.

One hundred and eighty before children
would make me two hundred years old
as I strolled the high school lawn, a perfect, June evening,

greeting neighbors at son Noah's graduation—
the morning after asking myself, perhaps,
what do I want from the next century and a half?

Maybe, a life like Lamech's of more than seven hundred summers,
winding like a river across a flat floodplain,
ample and relaxed enough

to leave pieces of itself behind
in cut-off, land-locked lakes—
muscled enough to coil tightly as a snake

so that at the end of a ten-hour day on its water,
someone like Meriwether Lewis
could walk across a quarter-mile of waist-high grass,

trying to get his land legs back,
and find himself on a piece of shore
he thought he'd left behind miles and hours before.

Enosh's span of nine hundred winters
would slow transience even more—
as does a winter with weeks below freezing

when water's flow stops, ice glints at the tops of trees,
and each hour in the woods
makes the idea of not being here, then being here,

then not being here again, more and more unlikely.
I think it was Thomas Merton who said
by the time you get to heaven there'll be little you left,

one way of testing what is and isn't holy—
whether it adds to or eases our sense of isolation,
of self existing apart from other, separate selves.

No use in hurrying to learn this lesson
today's snow and trees explain
with the same matter-of-factness

that reassured the nervous crowd in Yenan
when Mao Zedong proclaimed:
We have ten thousand years

to remake the culture and ourselves—
meaning, I think, that our first work
(before details of five year plans

to bump up lagging production)
is learning to trust history's unwinding,
and our own lives unwinding within it.

CHARLES WELD was educated at Cornell and the University of Maine and has worked as a mental health counselor in a variety of residential settings. Currently, he's employed as an administrator in a nonprofit agency serving children's mental health needs in central and western New York and lives in a village in the Finger Lakes region. His poetry has appeared in many small magazines. His chapbook, *Country I Would Settle In,* was published by Pudding House in 1994.

There Is Only the Dance

Time and Journey in T. S. Eliot

The things which are temporal arise by their participation in the things that are eternal.

—ALFRED NORTH WHITEHEAD

ALL RELIGIONS, AND ALL PHILOSOPHIES WITHOUT EXCEPTION, are concerned with the relations between the eternal and the temporal. Man has seen himself mythologically as part man, part god. In modern times, with secularization of thought being dominant, this mythological view has become somewhat eclipsed for no better reason than the current effort to interpret reality in purely temporal terms. Understanding the nature of our participation in matters eternal is, I feel, what is meant by the *journey*.

Of course, the states of temporality and eternity are entirely distinct, yet related to each other. Their relationship is best described in terms of dance or music. As I write this, what comes to mind are these lines from T. S. Eliot's *Four Quartets*:

At the still point of the turning world. Neither flesh
    nor fleshless;
Neither from nor towards; at the still point there the dance is,
But neither arrest nor movement. And do not call it fixity,
Where past and future are gathered. Neither movement from
    nor towards,
Neither ascent nor decline. Except for the point, the still point,
There would be no dance, and there is only the dance.

What is interesting about these lines is that they also spring from an attitude concerned with the relations of the temporal and the eternal; the same concern is found in several places throughout the poem:

> To apprehend the point of intersection of the timeless
>   with time...
> Here at the intersection of the timeless with time ...
> Here the impossible union of spheres of existence is actual ...

The co-existence of time and timeless is the puzzle at the heart of this poem, and it is in terms of *journey* that all aspects of time are explored: those that attempt to deal with this question and those that do not.

To understand how the temporal and the eternal relate to each other is concomitantly an exploration through our own lives of the relationship between heaven and earth, between earthly material and spiritual reality. Consequently, our attitude toward time is paramount. If one takes the attitude, for instance, that we only live once, that this is the only life, it often leads to a life of pure acquisition and constant gratification, for there is nothing other than the material life to motivate oneself. The concept of a moment, of a still point, becomes a fleeting thing, the specious moment, possessed of no lasting reality as the past moves into the inexorable future. Section three of Eliot's first movement, *Burnt Norton*, explores the implications of such a vastated perspective, in which the fleeting moment is a state of disaffection between the two poles of past and future, with no reference to the eternal. Here, our lives are described as though we are leaves blown in the wind:

> Men and bits of paper, whirled by the cold wind
> That blows before and after time.

Reading these lines, I am made mindful of his poem "The Wasteland," in which Eliot describes a similar attitude of mind driving people to work in much the same way:

> Unreal city,
> Under the brown fog of a winter dawn,
> A crowd flowed over London Bridge, so many,
> I had not thought death had undone so many.

The title of this poem is itself a mournful echo of what Swedenborg may have meant by *vastation,* and indeed, the last line cited above is taken from Dante's *Inferno,* which in itself has echoes in Swedenborg's *Heaven and Hell.* Far from being an objective observer to these events, Eliot was himself one of that crowd going to work everyday in the city to Lloyd's Bank. These are no abstract

Opposite:
Dancer.
Bronze, 5¼ in.,
Central Italy, Etruscan,
late Archaic Period,
about 500 B.C. Museum
of Fine Arts, Boston.
Museum purchase
with funds donated
by contribution.
Photograph © Museum
of Fine Arts, Boston.

thoughts, only his own feelings concerning his own experience, his journey.

Clearly, Eliot's journey is one that perceives the present moment, the moment of being where we are, as something crucial. It is during such moments—moments some writers have called epiphanies—that a clarity takes hold of one's mind and reverberates throughout the whole course of that person's life. But these moments are not necessarily what are often described as spiritual enlightenments. No, they are also moments of total undoing, when all that is held to be true and real suddenly evaporates beneath the significance of something indescribable. This contrast is stated by Eliot:

> Not the intense moment,
> Isolated, with no before or after,
> But a lifetime burning in every moment
> And not the lifetime of one man only
> But of old stones that cannot be deciphered.

This condition is where the real journey begins, when all that prepares us for life's journey is suddenly someone else's wisdom, not our own, which is imbued with their intentions and not ours. The moment of clarity—the wild thyme unseen, the winter lightning, the laughter in the garden, the music heard so deeply—all these things also lead to an undoing, and life's journey can become a hellish account of constant failures even among those things that are taken as successes.

In the devastated landscape of a London torn apart by bombs, Eliot is taken on a Dante-esque journey in which life's purpose reveals itself in a process of constant undoing rather than achievement. Here, at the point of death, where body and soul begin to separate, a life begins to perceive itself against a background of rage at human folly, and then comes the recognition of one's participation in it:

> And last, the rending pain of re-enactment
> Of all that you have done, and been; the shame
> Of motives late revealed, and the awareness
> Of things ill done and done to others' harm
> Which once you took as exercise of virtue.
> Then fool's approval stings and honour stains.

It is at this point of realization, in the middle of the process of vastation and devastation, that the real moment, the moment in and out of time, that reality reconfigures itself and remembers the non-tangible relation of man to myth—the dancer to the dance—as the only real source of salvation:

From wrong to wrong the exasperated spirit
Proceeds, unless restored by that refining fire
Where you must move in measure like a dancer.

This is the real key to the soulful journey, the refining fire and hence the process of purification. None of this will be unfamiliar to the reader of Swedenborg, in which this process is described in terms of regeneration. Key to this process is first of all the desire and the sense of lack and want for the truth, which by the time regeneration ends has inverted itself, and it is the desire to act from a sense of what is good that drives one forward. That point of inversion is also the point of greatest despair, for nothing remains to rescue us from our old lives that we can cling to for support and protection. In the earlier work, "The Wasteland," Eliot defines that moment in the most beautiful way:

> Datta: what have we given?
> My friend, blood shaking my heart
> The awful daring of a moment's surrender
> Which an age of prudence cannot retract
> By this, and this only, we have existed
> Which is not to be found in our obituaries
> Or in memories draped by the beneficent spider
> Or under seals broken by the lean solicitor
> In our empty rooms.

(*Datta* means *to give* from the Upanishads.) We measure our lives and the journeys undertaken in them by the things acquired and the differences our presence made to it. However, that which is truly given cannot be recorded and must be done unobserved if it is to have a genuine meaning. Is this not reminiscent of the widow's mite? What value is there in public acclaim or in the large or small empire we point to as evidence of our lives?

The moment—all the epiphanies that compose it—or even if it were only a single event, such as falling in love, changes our lives so completely that we come out of the experience as completely different people, yet outwardly unchanged. Nothing can ever be the same again, as every subsequent moment of our lives is filtered and measured through that moment. As each moment passes, so the whole of history is constantly altered and updated and puts to shame the rational idea of a static pile of knowledge that is to be passed on:

> There is, it seems to us,
> At best, only a limited value
> In the knowledge derived from experience.
> The knowledge imposes a pattern, and falsifies,
> For the pattern is new in every moment

And every moment is a new and shocking
Valuation of all we have been.

I have touched on very little in terms of the totality of what these poems mean. Nevertheless, I feel sure that my words resonate with the reader of Swedenborg. Eliot became a Christian late in life, much to the disapproval of his peers who saw it as rather unfashionable. It may well be that Eliot was familar with Swedenborg's writings, but I do not know. It is clear from what Eliot has written, however, that his journey in life was enriched by his profound perception of the eternal reality in relation to the temporal state—a very Swedenborgian concept. Contrasted to our purely modern temporal illusion that our journey is a constant running away, getting away from it all, of lotteries and insurances to protect us and guarantee no vastation, a life that acknowledges the presence of the eternal as part of its essential fabric is greatly enriched by it, not necessarily because it is made comfortable but quite the opposite. All lives are composed of their tragedies and burdens. If they were not, then it is because they are protected and thus incapable of the kind of sympathy and empathy that creates the desire to learn. But once we acknowledge our limitations, how little we can achieve on the basis of our own desires and designs, is it not then and only at such a point that the real journey truly begins?

After teaching for a number of years, KARL BIRJUKOV left that profession to explore poetry and philosophy. He says, "I feel as though I have travelled far from that place I was in as a teacher, and yet I have not been any place in the physical sense." His reviews and articles have appeared in various philosophical journals and his poetry in other publications. Since the early 1990s, he has written booklets and articles about the work of artist John Latham, which have accompanied the artist's exhibitions at institutions such as the Tate Gallery in London, the Museum of Modern Art in Oxford, and the Isaac Newton Institute in Cambridge. Currently he is writing a book, which combines philosophical, poetic, and scientific thought that demonstrates the relevance of Swedenborg to the modern world. He lives in London.

MARIANNE TAYLOR

Mid-day at the Museum

Eastern Art Gallery

Another stony virgin
sits stiffly, this Byzantine
queen holds a miniature
boy, also of stone
no petal soft infant
smelling of milk and
talcum; even now
his long, thin fingers
and narrow instep re-
semble those of the man
on the cross. Is that
why? Is the death
the purpose, after all?

All these wizened
Eastern infants seem
to agree, yet my
small son in his
upholstered stroller
digs in his heels and squirms
around to look at me,
offering a triumphant
plump fist of raisins, sweet
sun-darkened fruit
of the vine, of the earth.

I bend to receive them.

MARIANNE TAYLOR is a professor of English at Kirkwood Community College. She was the first-place winner of the 2004 Allen Ginsberg Award. Her book, *Salt Water, Iowa,* has been a finalist in two competitions, and she has been published widely in national journals, such as *North America Review, Alaska Quarterly Review, Connecticut Review,* and *Rosebud.* She lives in Mount Vernon, Iowa, with her husband and four sons.

Chocolat Religieuse

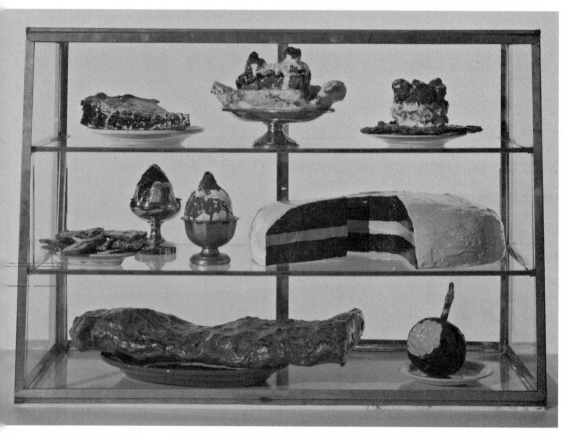

Claes Oldenburg.
Pastry Case I.
Enamel paint on nine plaster sculptures in glass showcase, 20¾ x 30⅛ x 14¾ in., 1961–1962.
The Museum of Modern Art, New York, New York.
The Sidney and Harriet Janis Collection. Digital image © The Museum of Modern Art/Licensed by SCALA/Art Resource, New York.

I THOUGHT I HAD GONE TO PARIS to see the *Mona Lisa* or stroll along the Champs Elyseés; in truth, I went for the pastry. I didn't realize my desire until the flakey pastry was in my mouth—melting. It was much the same way one discovers the meaning of having a body, suddenly and by surprise, in the presence of a lover. In Paris, I spent many little minutes of delicious days, concocting in my imagination the exact texture of the tartine of my dreams: ratios among crème, chocolate, and delicate pastry. When I wasn't counting metro stops, I plotted my next fresh moments of consummation—which patisserie, which tart, and when. As it turned out, the same day I had the pleasure of consuming the most perfect confection of my life—the "chocolat religieuse," the voluptuous older cousin of the chocolate éclair from a little patisserie in the thirteenth arrondissement—was the day I was shocked into awareness of my own mortality.

BEFORE THE PASTRY, I VISITED THE CATACOMBS. I was with Jeanne, my teacher friend. At first, the subterranean sepulcher felt like a well-done haunted house at a fair—we shrieked and giggled, but the preponderance of death sobered us: it was bones, bones, bones and more bones—six million sculls and skeletons taken from medieval cemeteries and arranged into 4-foot walls that went on and on and on. In some places, the heads made the shape of crosses. Although I didn't overtly cringe, I made sure I didn't lean against the bones or brush my hand across them as I passed. Trying to activate our rationality, we translated the stone placards. Many were reassurances of life after death. Some were ominous, like the one that said, "Death is a blind monster who will eventually kill all."

Surrounded by skulls and skeletons, my own mortality blew through me like a wind through cotton. As all who have worn a mortal coil, I too would shuffle off my flesh, my bones. It occurred to me, as a student of Buddhism, that perhaps my soul had once worn those very bones in some medieval incarnation . . . I thought of the dead wishing for a tart au fraises, a chocolate, a sweet kiss on the lips, soft, sincere, the breath of a lover's voice in their ear. Here, their desires seemed absurd. Those desires kept us locked in the catacombs of this earth, reincarnating again and again to eat, drink, fornicate, and chase chimeras until once again our bones became dust.

I hadn't realized how tense I was until we emerged from the tunnels into the sunlight, and I relaxed my shoulders again.

"I have to say, that was kind of disturbing," admitted Jeanne.

We walked silently for half a block.

"Where to now?" Jeanne asked.

"Why don't we find some pastries?" I suggested.

Here Jeanne scrunched up her forehead. "I'm focusing on homeless people and the pastries, the crêpes—it's just too much."

The summer before, Jeanne had taken me on an expedition in a dugout canoe to visit a remote indigenous tribe in Nicaragua. There, the children had stomachs bloated from malnutrition. As a result of the hurricane, the tribe crammed eighteen people into each makeshift bamboo hut. We brought them Tylenol, Pepto Bismal, pencils, and Bic pens, plus a little money for more supplies. The children picked up the broken pencil leads that fell on the ground thinking they were seeds. Nicaragua was Jeanne's choice; Paris, mine. In Paris, Jeanne empathized with the homeless and struggled with my hedonistic obsession with pastries and Nutella crêpes. That day on the street after we emerged from the catacombs, she said she would take a walk by herself: she needed to be alone. That would be better for both of us.

I went on a quest for the perfect pastry. At the moment, I had little interest in bothering myself with homelessness or *Hurricane Mitch*. Eating pastries would not obliterate world hunger or make me immortal—I knew this. I was just thankful to have a body coursing with life. Each tartine was an invitation to revel in that life.

I could tell by the name, *chocolat religieuse*, that the pastry I found was exactly what I was looking for. The people in the patisserie put it in a white paper bag, which I carried until I came to a park that was sufficiently lovely, with trees and a fountain. Before I ate the pastry, I photographed it. I am not sure if I have ever been as present during the consumption of a dessert as I was during the *chocolat religieuse*. The sun sparkled on the water in the fountain. The crème was elevated, the chocolate authoritative yet subtle and eminently satisfying. I thought: I am too romantic to be unhappy. Certainly, I am not unflawed, but I am also not unholy. If I wrote romance novels, they would be embarrassing—too extravagant. That is the way I love to live—swimming in large, embarrassing, delicious pools of happiness.

Later, that evening, I went to a café and thought. The waiter who brought me the café au lait asked if I was thinking about him. Of course, I said, but thought about bones and watched the streetlights reflect in puddles outside. . . . As it boasted, the monster of death would indeed claim all, but we also would escape because we are more than just bones. We are not mere tongues and bowels. We are *l'esprit eternal*. We are *Winged Victory*, like the statue at the Louvre. Why, by the way, does she have no head? Arms, legs, breasts, wings and a heart—perhaps a brain is the treacherous organ which pledges to satisfy but instead gives numbers, words, plans and does not fulfill its promises of truth, good, or beauty. We are more than mere brains. Zen Buddhists know this because, after all, the sound of one hand clapping is the hush one hears when one is still and knows God. When the body is dust, a spark remains. With some gray hair and a few wrinkles, I felt sexy—ready to be tossed and lost and broken by the fearful joy that spins universes in and out of existence. I craved sweets, men, God—I knew that I would find them all, eventually, in this life or the next. In fact, I had already found a most ideal pastry.

SARAH CLOWES lives in Minneapolis with her husband and teaches reading at Minneapolis Community and Technical College. She enjoys meditation and pastry.

A Passport
for Archie

ALICE ARCHER SEWALL (1870–1955) and her four younger sisters—
Maude, Mary (Maidy), Rachel (Rae), and Elizabeth (Bess)—spent
their childhood in the small Ohio town of Urbana. In 1886, her family left Urbana for Scotland, where her father, Frank Sewall, was to
serve as interim pastor to a Glasgow Swedenborgian society. Archie
looked forward to visiting places already familiar from her father's
stories of trips abroad after he had graduated from Bowdoin College.

In Glasgow, Archie and her sister Maude, then sixteen and fourteen, continued their education under their father's tutelage, reading
Cicero and Virgil in Latin and studying British history, philosophers,
poets, and novelists. At a time when many art schools admitted only
men, Archie enrolled in the Glasgow School of Art, where all classes
except life drawing were open to women. Since there were many
"new" women among Glasgow artists, Archie probably absorbed
some of their emancipated attitudes as she developed her own career.

At the conclusion of his Glasgow pastorate, Frank Sewall took his
wife and five daughters to the continent for a year of travel. Wherever
they went, there was thoughtful preparation for what they would see.
Often Archie regaled her sisters with bedtime stories about events
that had taken place in the locale they were to visit the next day, stories so vivid that the young tourists could "see the blood on the stairs."
As they travelled, the girls learned history, literature, and languages,
lessons that remained vivid in their minds throughout their lives.

Quotations from Archie's memoirs are drawn from "Memoir of My Education," written
in 1946 as part of Archie's application for a Guggenheim fellowship.

The girls were expected to write about their travels, and each of them was given a sketchbook and told to paint. Archie's sketchbook, entitled *Through the Alps and Northern Italy* was dated Summer 1888 and contains sketches and watercolors of castles, cathedrals, and scenic vistas, some painted in and around Florence in Spring 1889.

Archie was most impressed by the museums—the British Museum where she "met the Greeks," Florence where she "painted copies incessantly," Rome where she "came under the magnificence of the serene Raphael, which to me has never been disturbed." In describing Italy, she noted, "the intense individualism of every city and village, the beauty of line and its utter expressiveness, whether in manuscript, fresco, or in bas-relief, or up-leading towers." Music was also part of the cultural riches. Archie records:

> We settled somewhere near the door of Wagner's Bayreuth theatre for awhile and became engrossed in *Parsifal* and *Siegfried*. Maude taught us the dramatic motifs from the little parlour organ in our boarding house, and we practiced them walking through the meadow to the performance. Of course, in Dresden, the great orchestra met us again, the whole of the Niebelungen Ring; all the Beethoven symphonies poured out to us, sitting on the terrace above the river.

Inevitably the children picked up signals that there was something unusual about their family. Many stories from these days in Europe were told to the daughter of Mary, Archie's sister. Mary's daughter recalled, "When walking in Europe, they must have walked in a row, for my mother overheard a stranger say, "One, two, three, four, five, six, seven, . . . counting off the Sewalls as they walked along." No doubt the exuberance of Frank Sewall caught attention, and the sight of a family absorbed in sharing his appreciation of the sights and culture of Europe must have been noteworthy.

Frank Sewall, whom Archie called "an artist in life," had a sense of ceremony and timing. He chose books for the family to read, in their original languages, according to places that would bring them alive. Archie remembers reading "The Lake poets . . . as we dawdled down the lanes around Nab Cottage. . . . Somewhere between Pisa and Milan and on our way to Venice, we read the whole of Faust, both parts. In the villages of the Tyrol we read Herman and Dorothea." Archie also attributes to her father a sense of selection, of determining what not to do, as she recalls the family visit to France:

> It might have been with me in mind that our weeks in Paris were spent in the great palaces and gardens, some evenings at the opera, some society among New Church friends, but no dallying as in other cities among people on the bridges and in odd corners of history. Knowing as I do from later observa-

Joseph Cornell. *Medici Princess.* Painted wood, photo-mechancial reproductions, painted and colored glass, painted paper, string, cork, metal rings, plastic balls, and a feather in a glass-faced painted wood box, 17⅝ x 12¼ x 4¾ in., ca. 1952. Hirshhorn Museum and Sculpture Garden, Smithsonian Institution. Museum Purchase, 1979.

tions, testimonies, and reading, what the basis was for the natural dread of the Latin Quarter in the minds of many good parents of gifted youths in that day, I can believe he did not want the pull of the great technique to set in upon me. Certain it was that he passed by the outstanding invitation of the finest school in the world in silence, and took his little flock to Florence. But, no doubt in answer to his prayers, I would yet receive the Beaux Arts training in another way.

As Archie describes it, there was "a perpetual sunniness in which we went about the world," even on rainy days, which were "wonderful, more so if a little chilly, needing inventions—rugs or sticks in the stove, etc.—for comfort. Huddled together we could chuckle more and read better." She attributes this perpetual sunniness to being "grounded in the laws of truth and rectitude" which "flow from the celestial principle," meaning that living according to divine order creates a positive and joyous approach to life. This sense of joy permeated Frank Sewall's life, to the point where he once told Archie, "My name should have been Felix. Frank is a good name, but it does not fully express my life as Felix would have—it has been so very happy."

After three years in Europe, when Frank Sewall accepted a call to become pastor of the Swedenborgian Church in Washington, D.C., the scene of Archie's education shifted back to America. Although she had little experience with schools, Archie returned to America as a well-educated young woman. She had learned art history at its sources, absorbed a broad background in the culture and literature of Europe, knew German, Italian, French, and Latin, and studied philosophy and Swedenborg with her father. Her schooling, shared with her sister Maude, had been personalized in a way that permitted her own unique enthusiasms and prompted individual inquiry. Although she earned no grades, wrote no term papers, and had no rank in a class nor school transcript, her mind had been trained, her capacities for scholarship honed, and an intellectual companionship with her father established—benefits destined to have far-reaching consequences in her life.

ALICE BLACKMER SKINNER is a research psychologist who specializes in the study of the lives of women. This essay is abridged from the second chapter of "Stay By Me Roses," Dr. Skinner's study of Alice Archer Sewall James, a manuscript in process. Like Archie, Alice Skinner also lived in Urbana, Ohio, in her early childhood.

What We Learn from Flint

These little hills that roll so gently down
toward the Scioto, how often I have traced
their backs with a willow switch,
scouring the furrows for arrowheads—

old miracles of craft and trade
some other young man made and used,
then lost, someone who must have loved
the way these locusts bloom in April.

When our plows had turned the washes,
and hard May rains had knocked apart the clods,
I could fill my hands with chips of flint—
a pocketful of history on a sunny afternoon—

and know that other feet had walked these hills.
Such thoughts folded the time in a way
that I have not expanded since,
the way pale horizons disappear

when you kneel on a ridge and flip up
a spear point, just where it dropped centuries ago.
Millennia rush like floods over bottom ground
and suddenly we're scholars of the heart.

William Jolliff, a native of Magnetic Springs, Ohio, teaches English at George Fox University. His poetry has appeared in many journals, including *West Branch*, *Midwest Quarterly*, *Northwest Review*, and *Southern Humanities Review*. He is also a songwriter, and his *Laughlin Boy*, recorded by Tracy Grammer, was the fourth most-played song on American folk radio in 2005.

Safe Passage through Nepal

The Everest Massif and Ama Dablam viewed from Shyangboche above Namche.

*"there is something in man which responds
to the challenge of this mountain . . . the struggle is
the struggle of life itself upward and forever upward"*
—GEORGE MALLORY

THE HIGHEST MOUNTAINS ON EARTH are within the Himalayan range, and eight of the ten highest mountains are in the small country of Nepal. Nepal is landlocked between China and India and has experienced the pressure of a small neighbor squeezed between two giants. Mount Everest is called Chomolungma, mother goddess, by the Sherpa people, who, according to ethnographers, came from Tibet over five-hundred years ago to settle in the high-altitude region of northeastern Nepal. The Sherpas brought Tibetan culture and Buddhism with them. Most Nepalese in the lower altitudes are Hindu and recognize a kinship with India.

In 1995 I did an "introductory" one-week trek in the Khumbu region of Nepal, hiking and camping along the Mt. Everest base camp trail and visiting Sherpa villages and Buddhist monasteries. The Nepalese people are friendly, courageous, and sensitive. I am not

Buddhist or Hindu, but I responded to the spiritual aesthetics of thanka paintings, prayer flags, and chanting monks in the Buddhist gompas, and I enjoyed hearing the stories of the Hindu gods and heroes. There is wisdom in storytelling, and there is soulfulness in the discipline of mantra chanting unknown to, or forgotten by, most of my Christian brethren.

In 1999, the U.S. State Department began withdrawing embassy personnel from Nepal due to increasing political instability, and travelers were warned to stay away. My reluctance to return, however, was more personal. Mountaineering is a perilous form of adventure. In 1995 an entire group of Japanese trekkers as well as many local Sherpas were killed by an avalanche. I had made friends with the Japanese group two days before they were killed. In 1999 three porters were killed by an avalanche on a ridge above my climbing team. I escaped physical injury but not the emotional scarring left by helplessly seeing people disappear into a white abyss. After that, I just did not want to be cold, wet, exhausted, or scared again. I thought I'd had enough of mountaineering, but in 2003 the attraction to celebrate the fiftieth anniversary of the first summit of Mt. Everest with other mountaineers was too great. So I returned, and then again in 2004, and mostly recently in 2006.

In my research of Nepalese guiding companies for the 2006 expedition, I discovered Adventure Geo Treks and became friends by e-mail with the owner, Niru Rai. Niru and I worked out an itinerary for a group of seven trekkers and novice climbers to arrive in Nepal on April 28, 2006. The plan was to spend a few days in Katmandu, and then do a fifteen-day trek through the Khumbu region and climb Lobuche East, a peak just southwest of Mt. Everest.

Unfortunately, after our reservations were made, political unrest in Nepal reached a crescendo. Massive demonstrations had broken out against the government. The military and police were shooting demonstrators in the streets of the capital, Katmandu. We began to fear that we would arrive in a country on the brink of civil war. Two members of our group canceled, leaving only five of us—Greg and Bill from Indiana, and Vitto and Mark (Americans living overseas in Singapore and Tokyo), and me.

Nepal has a stormy political history and only brief periods of democracy. In 2001 the well-liked King Birendra and nine members of the royal family were massacred, and the king's younger brother, Gyanendra, was crowned. King Gyanendra's rule became increasingly authoritarian and less democratic as he limited civil rights and dismissed Parliament. In April 2006, shortly before our arrival, hundreds of thousands of Nepalese again took to the streets of Katmandu to demonstrate against the monarchy.

Fate was, nevertheless, kind to us. Our group of five middle-aged American men arrived two days after King Gyanendra withdrew his order of martial law, restored the constitution, and recalled Parliament. The major democratic parties and the Maoists agreed to participate in elections to be held in the fall, and the Maoists declared a ninety-day truce. We were, thus, surprised and delighted to find a people thrilled with the restoration of democracy and the prospect of a lasting peace. Major challenges are yet to be faced, however, as conversations with Nepalese revealed deep distrust of the king and worries over how the Maoists will be integrated into the political process.

When we landed in Katmandu, there were fewer police and military on the streets than when I had last been there in October 2004. There were also far fewer Westerners in Katmandu and in the mountains. Other than a few intrepid Israelis, we were the only non-locals on most of the trails we hiked. With fewer trekkers on the trails, narrow bridge crossings were quicker and easier.

After settling in at the Katmandu Guest House in Thamel, the old town of Katmandu, we spent a couple of days sightseeing. We viewed cremations at Pashupati on the banks of the Baghmati, ate lunch overlooking the giant stupa at Bouddhanath, and walked among the monkeys in the high temples and stupas of Swoyambho.

Stupas are Buddhist monuments with symbolic architecture representing Buddhist cosmology and are intended to remind followers of the path of enlightenment. In Nepal they are white-washed hemispheric-domed structures, like an overturned bowl, with the all-seeing eyes of Buddha painted on the four sides of a rectangular tower atop the white dome. Above the tower is a gold spire with thirteen segments representing the thirteen stages of Buddhahood. On top of the spire is a crescent moon and spike symbolizing the truth of Buddha's teaching as the light above the earth and sky. Smaller versions of stupas are found in many Nepalese villages and local sacred places, and are called chortens. The last historical incarnation of Buddha was born in Lumbini in southern Nepal. Prince Siddharta Gautama (563–483 BC) was the heir of a royal family. The prince renounced his royal inheritance to lead an ascetic life and seek enlightenment. He became Sakyamuni Buddha, the Buddha of recorded human history, after he reached enlightenment and his consciousness became one with the Godhead. According to tradition, the remains of Sakymuni Buddha were cremated and the ashes divided and buried under eight stupas in India. His followers circled the stupas meditating and chanting, as they still do today at the great stupa of Bouddhanath in Katmandu and around chortens in villages high up in the Khumbu.

We flew up into the high Himalaya and landed on the airstrip in the Sherpa village of Lukla, where the Mount Everest base camp trail begins. The views from the twin-prop plane are spectacular, and the landing is always a thrill as the runway begins above a sheer drop-off of hundreds of feet and ends at an equally sheer cliff-face. There is no room for pilot error.

In Lukla we met up with our crew of porters, cook and kitchen staff, sirdar (chief guide), and climbing guide, seventeen in all, who would tend to our needs over the next fifteen days of hiking, camping, and climbing. Nepal expedition companies run treks and mountaineering expeditions in the British tradition, meaning that clients will engage in challenging hiking or climbing but will be well fed and sheltered in sturdy tents and warm sleeping bags at night. While our porters carried 60 to 80 lbs. of supplies up steep and hazardous trails, we carried only daypacks with as much or as little as we chose. Each morning we were awakened with hot tea brought to our tents, along with warm water in a washing bowl for our face and hands.

The Everest base camp trail snakes north out of Lukla (9,184 ft.) winding its way through the Khumbu region to Sherpa villages, monasteries, and yak pastures across glacier-fed rivers on plank and cable suspension bridges. Most stages of the trail were originally established by yak herders and Tibetan traders. The trail terminus at the current base camp for Mt. Everest climbing expeditions is at 17,594 feet altitude.

In Namche Bazaar (11,286 ft.), the central village of the Khumbu, we visited the honorary mayor, Gheylsan Sherpa. Gheylsan served as one of the high-altitude porters on the first summit of Mt. Everest in 1953 by Tenzing Norgay and Edmund Hillary. I met and interviewed Gheylsan in May 2003 for an article I was researching. I gave him a copy of the April 2003 edition of *Outside* magazine, which he had not seen, but which had his picture on the cover. He still had the magazine on his eating table when we visited in May 2006. His family was

Mani stones and the all-seeing eyes of Buddha are found at this stupa outside Debuche, less than a mile from Tengboche. Mani stones are inscribed with Buddhist prayers.

Trekkers headed for the Mt. Everest region usually spend a rest day or two in the Sherpa village of Namche Bazaar. The village is a major regional trading center.

delighted with our visit and served us salted yak butter tea (which we politely choked down) and cookies. Gheylsan and his wife are old for Sherpas (late eighties in a country with an average lifespan of fifty). His eyes were clear and his voice strong, but he'd developed hearing problems since my visit in 2003.

During our "rest day" in Namche, Ganesh led us on a four-hour hike to Khumjung, which, with a population of over 1,000, is the largest Sherpa village in Nepal. We gave donations to its monastery, viewed the monastery's famous/infamous Yeti skull ("snow valley man" in Tibetan, supposedly related to the North American "Big Foot"), and visited the first Hillary school in the Khumbu for Sherpa children. Sir Edmund Hillary is revered by the Sherpas because he founded the Himalayan Trust to help the Sherpa people of Nepal build schools and hospitals in the Khumbu.

The next day we branched off the main trail onto a trail new to me—the Gokyo trail. The altitude and wear on middle-aged bodies began taking their toll on our group. Greg developed severe cold-like symptoms and migraines, and I started suffering pressure headaches. Greg and I spent a recovery day in the stream-side village of Machermo, while the others trekked on to Gokyo.

The following morning, Bill, Mark, and Vitto hiked to the top of Gokyo Ri (17,581 ft). Greg and I caught up with them at the beautiful, blue glacial lakes of Gokyo—water on top of the world.

We camped in a yak pasture called Dragnag the following night. Vitto confessed over breakfast that he'd acquired a severe case of yak-phobia. He'd spent the entire night with a trekking pole in his hand convinced that a giant yak would break through his tent and gore him. The domesticated yak, along with its cross-bred relative the dzopkyo (usually called "dzo"), is the foundation of the Sherpa economy, providing food (milk, cheese, and meat), clothing and fiber for yarn, and transportation of goods over mountain passes. Yak dung is the primary source of fuel for villagers living above the tree line. Western sensibilities are usually challenged the first time a trekker sees a Sherpani (Sherpa woman) collecting yak dung along the trail and pressing it into patties with her hands. But yak dung burns with a sweet, pungent smell and has kept many trekkers warm in Sherpa teahouses and lodges.

In the morning we climbed up the Cho La, one of the highest and steepest passes in the region (17,482 feet). I developed a sinus infection that sapped my strength, and I had a very difficult time making it over the pass. Our cook, Dorge, showed great patience and sensitivity by staying near me as I struggled to the top of the pass without humiliating me with offers of assistance.

We were tested severely with two very long and difficult days of high altitude hiking and scramble climbing up and over rocky passes. Mark, a reserve colonel in the U.S. Marine Corps, informed us that the two days were the most physically challenging of his life and more difficult than boot camp. When asked how hard it would be to climb Lobuche East, Ganesh replied with a cheery laugh that it would be at least 150-percent harder than Cho La. Mark and Vitto decided that their goal to experience the Himalayas had been met, and they preferred to pass on attempting the climb. In the morning they trekked out with our climbing guide, Norbu, and two porters to head back to Lukla. Bill had not intended to attempt the climb of Lobuche, so he took our English-speaking porter, Gopal, and headed up to Everest base camp. Greg and I decided we would lower our sights from Lobuche East (20,070 feet), since we both had colds, to the less difficult Pokalde Peak (19,044 feet), which I had climbed in 1998.

TO REACH POKALDE BASE CAMP, our remaining crew, Greg, and I had to hike east from the Base Camp Trail and scramble up yet a higher pass, Kongma La (18,155 feet). Ganesh tied prayer flags at the top of the pass and led the porters in doing puja, asking for the blessing of safety for all of us in the mountains and our families at home. Prayer flags are colorful cloth rectangles decorated with Tibetan Buddhist religious symbols and prayers. They are strung on cords and tied to boulders on high passes and peaks, and it is believed that when they blow in the wind, prayers are offered up to deities to benefit those who hung them and others who show respect. Puja is the Hindu ritual of chanting prayers and making food offerings to gods. Devout Hindus typically perform Puja at least once each day. Ganesh and our crew of porters are Rai, which are a "middle people" in Nepal; meaning they live below the high-mountain dwelling Sherpa-Buddhists and above the predominantly Hindu people of the valleys. Many Rai, including our crew, practice both Hinduism and Buddhism.

In the morning Greg decided not to chance it, so Ganesh and I began the climb up Pokalde at sunrise. We were the only ones on the mountain. It was partly cloudy, so our views of the Everest Massif, just a few miles north, and the other mountain peaks in the area were disappointing. But the final sixty feet of free climbing rock at over 19,000 feet was one hell of an adrenaline rush.

I collapsed into my tent totally exhausted after our descent, requesting only a wash bowl and puke pan. I wanted to lie in my tent the rest of the day, but, unfortunately, our climbing permit was for Lobuche, not Pokalde, and another team had come over the Kongma La to set up a base camp at Pokalde. So, Ganesh wanted to break camp and depart before the other group came over to our camp asking questions. We could be fined, and Ganesh's guiding license would be at risk for climbing Pokalde without a permit. After only a half-hour rest we hurriedly broke camp and began the trek out to Dengboche village.

Ganesh and I fell behind the rest of our crew as I was laboring at such a slow pace. We got lost in dense fog and had to navigate by listening for the roar of the rushing Imja Khola River, fed by the glacier runoff from Everest. What should have been a 3.5-hour descent to Dengboche turned into 5 hours, as we blindly picked our way down rocky slopes.

Reunited with Bill and Gopal in Dengboche, the next day we trekked through a vast blooming rhododendron forest to the Buddhist convent at Debuche and then up to Tengboche Monastery, where we camped on the grounds. From the monastery, the view of the majestic white peaks of the great mountains of the Khumbu, Everest, Lhotse, Lhotse Shar, Nuptse, Ama Dablam, Pumo Ri, Tawache, Thamserku and others is awe inspiring.

In the morning Ganesh and I obtained a private audience with the High Lama Rimpoche Tenzing, who presides over Tengboche Monastery and is the most revered religious leader of the Sherpa people. Lama Tenzing spent an hour in conversation with me (Ganesh interpreting). When asked what message I might take from him to friends in the U.S., he replied, "Tell everyone to cultivate love in their hearts. Tell the truth. Promote love in the heart and truth-telling through religious discipline."

Our hike back to Lukla ended with the last hour in pouring rain, a good sign that it was time to go home. We had a final night in a lodge with hot showers and a last dinner with our crew. Dancing and singing were led by Norbu, who can sing a hundred different verses of *"Resper, resper, resperee, sometimes monkey, sometimes donkey . . ."*

Back in Katmandu we reunited with Sangha for more sightseeing in the temple cities of the Katmandu Valley. Our last dinner was at Niru Rai's house with his family, Ganesh, and Sangha. The feast consisted of too many courses to count and many glasses of Mrs. Niru's home-brewed rakshi. Afterwards, Bill and I walked the darkened streets of Thamel one last time and treated ourselves to a Guinness at Thamel's "authentic" Irish pub.

NEPAL HAS PASSED THROUGH A VIOLENT TIME IN ITS HISTORY, and the passage may not yet be completed. I have found it difficult to accept that thousands of Nepalese have died violent deaths during the Maoist insurgency and military crackdown because of my own experience of Nepal as a place of peace and kindness to the stranger. Greeting in Nepal is "namaste," usually translated as, "I recognize the god in you." I hope that the Nepalese will recognize the god in each other across political lines. May God grant safe passage to Nepal.

JEFF RASLEY holds a master's degree in divinity from Christian Theological Seminary, a law degree from Indiana University, and a bachelor of arts degree from the University of Chicago where he majored in philosophy, religion, and politics. He lives in Indianapolis, where he is a practicing lawyer, when he is not practicing his other calling of world travel and adventure. All the photographs are by the author.

When we reached Kongma La, an 18,155-foot pass east of Lobuche, Ganesh and the porters prepared for the Hindu ritual of puja.

LINDA PASTAN

Another Spring

They come like recurring dreams—
another spring, and another—
so many colored beads on an abacus
and all identical. And if we
are different each year,

if time seems to press
its thumbprint not on a laurel stem
or plum branch but only
on the backs of our own hands,
smooth once but ridged now

as the most veined of leaves,
must we take comfort in this?
Should we stop counting and simply
let ourselves fall into this dream
of perfect weather?

LINDA PASTAN's twelfth book of poems, *Queen of a Rainy Country,* will be published by Norton in October. She served as Poet Laureate of Maryland from 1991 to 1995 and was the winner of the 2003 Ruth Lilly Prize.

PART II

Breaking Out

One morning, waking, I understand that
much life lies behind me, so far back
on the road that I can no longer see it.

—THOMAS R. SMITH, THE ROAD (p. xi)
See also *Secrets of Heaven* 8961, Swedenborg (p. 161).

WAYNE CARHART

Widowhood

MR. AND MRS. CARLSON WERE OUR ACROSS-THE-STREET NEIGHBORS.
They had two boys, George Jr. and Richard. The Carlsons lived as
their neighbors lived, and their house was like their neighbors' houses. Mrs. Carlson was a stay-at-home housewife, and Mr. Carlson was
an adjuster for Allstate Insurance Company. "They're just like us," the
neighbors said.

The Carlsons took their parenting responsibilities seriously.
Although Mrs. Carlson was trained as a music teacher, she had not
taught since her marriage, devoting most of her time to house cleaning, being a den mother, and tending her modest flower garden.
Occasionally, in the summertime when the windows were open, we
could hear her playing the baby grand piano in the sunporch of their
home. Mr. Carlson, like other fathers in the neighborhood, was active in sports with his boys. During his two-week vacation, he traveled with his family to one of the national parks, always packing their
Nash sedan the night before the trip and leaving very early the next

Andrew Wyeth.
Wind from the Sea.
Tempera,
18.5 x 27.5 in., 1947.
Mead Art Museum,
Amherst College,
Massachusetts.
Gift from the Estate
of Charles E. Morgan.
©Andrew Wyeth.

49

morning. "You couldn't want for better neighbors than Ruth and George," the neighbors said.

After Richard and George Jr. had grown and left home, Mrs. Carlson took occasional substitute teaching jobs. I remember she taught me a few times. No matter what subject was assigned, she always turned the class into a sing-a-long. In biology class she would pass out song sheets, change our seating according to our voice pitch, whip out a recorder from her purse, and lead us into song. She was able to get even the most pseudo-sophisticated fourteen-year-old to join. "Our youngsters like it when Mrs. Carlson teaches," the parents said.

When I left the neighborhood for college, I gave little thought to the Carlsons until a letter from my mother told me that Mr. Carlson had died of a heart attack. My mother was sorry and I, too, had a sense of loss, but not one that lingered, for I was caught up in college life. "How sad, just when he could enjoy his retirement," the neighbors said.

Then another letter came telling me the neighborhood was all abuzz over Mrs. Carlson. "She's flipped out," the neighbors said. You see, soon after the death of her husband, she sold their new DeSoto and purchased one of those Volkswagen bugs. "Why a convertible and why red? What was wrong with the DeSoto? Why, it was this year's model."

Mrs. Carlson's next move was to convert half of her garage into a music studio with a greenhouse extension. She had traditional spring flowers in full bloom starting in January, and she could be seen working with her plants well into the evening. "Why would she do that?" neighbors asked.

Of course, no one ever asked Mrs. Carlson those questions. My mother started to include a Ruth Carlson update written in the style of a newspaper gossip column in her weekly letter. Those dispatches were fun to read, especially when she reported that Mrs. Carlson had dyed her hair blonde and that she left her house each evening around 6 PM. She drove her red convertible to the railroad station and boarded a train for New York City. No one knew her destination, and no one asked, but the neighbors had their own ideas.

As each new theory was put forth, mother reported it in her weekly letter/column. The most benign idea was that she was going alone to concerts at the newly opened Lincoln Center. Some thought she had a terminal disease and was getting treatment at one of the city's medical centers, but she looked too healthy and happy. Besides, she returned much too late for that. The most common speculation was that Mrs. Carlson was having an affair. Of course, comments held that if it was an affair, it was too soon after Mr. Carlson's death. "She must have known him before George's death," they guessed. "Whatever the reason for the trips, it must be a good one. Why would anyone want to take that awful train into the city?" Mrs. Jackson, our next door neighbor, said.

Then came reports that Mrs. Carlson started playing her piano early in the morning. She had moved it to the studio portion of her garage. But she no longer played Bach, Mozart, or Telleman. Show tunes and popular songs like "Tenderly" and "September Song" wafted from the studio, and neighbors said, over and over again, "What in the world is going on?"

There came a letter from my mother—the second in only one week—with FLASH! printed across the top. Pasted to the stationery was a clipping from the *New York Herald Tribune,* a review of Ruthie Carlson's performance at the piano bar of the Hotel Astor, just off Times Square.

> Ruthie Carlson draws a crowd three-deep around her white piano every night. No night is complete without several requests for her rendition of "September Song," that she sings with her sweet and longing voice, "It's a long long time from May to December." Ruthie Carlson is someone you want to spend some time with at the Hotel Astor's piano bar.

I'll never know if any of Mrs. Carlson's other neighbors ventured into Times Square to witness this phenomenon or what they may have said. I can only report that on the night of my pilgrimage, I recognized no one except Mrs. Carlson herself. I found a small table close to the piano and ordered a scotch on the rocks, exercising my freshly acquired privilege to imbibe, and surveyed the middle-aged crowd. Some were out-of-towners, but most seemed to be regulars, all enjoying themselves. The one who seemed the happiest, however, was Ruthie Carlson. When my eyes finally met hers, I was surprised not so much with her twinkle of recognition, despite my new bohemian goatee, but with the sound of my own voice. I was part of this crowd—my now young adult pseudo-sophistication melting away, as Ruthie Carlson, a.k.a. Mrs. Carlson, my neighbor, led us all like some high-school class of days gone by through her haunting rendition of "September Song."

WAYNE CARHART is a retired health administrator. His last position was director of Family Court Mental Health Services for New York City. His lifelong interest in history and the idiosyncrasies of people and the way they choose to live their lives are reflected in his writing. After moving to Vermont in 1997, Carhart served as president of the Brattleboro Historical Society. A collection of his monthly newspaper articles on Brattleboro's history is soon to be published by the Brattleboro Area Chamber of Commerce to commemorate its one-hundredth anniversary. Carhart is currently working on a novel about his chance meeting with the actor Hurd Hatfield.

Changing Skins

It takes so much time
to pull it off.
A biting of your own tail,
whiplash turns in tight places.

Life above your head becomes
mere distraction to brush off.
A mouse could walk across
your nose and you wouldn't
even look up.   Finally

the last piece rips free.   Suddenly
you're that full of light
you might even swallow the sky.

Your new skin
shiny with surprise
is perfect in its marking,

an unexpected
meeting of yourself again,
a hiss, a flick of the tongue
tasting the air.

LYNN MARTIN's poetry has appeared in *Calliope, River City Review, South Florida Review, The Garden State, Green Mountains Review, Sinister Wisdom, 5 a.m., Connecticut Review, Earth's Daughters, Ancient Mariners, Out in the Mountains, Bloodstone, Sweet Annie Press, The Centennial Review,* and *Friend's Journal,* and in the anthologies *Heartbeat of New England* (2000) and *My lover is a woman* (1996). Her nonfiction has been published in *Mystery Review* (Spring 2000). Lynn was recently honored in Washington, D.C., for her work in the AIDS epidemic by a national organization called Experience Works, Prime Time Awards.

PHAYVANH LUEKHAMHAN

Escape from Laos

David Diao.
History Lessons.
Acrylic on canvas,
85 x 66 in., 1980.
Albright-Knox Art Gallery,
Buffalo, New York.
Charles Clifton
Fund, 1981.

ALL I'VE EVER KNOWN IS AMERICA—that's not true—what I remember is America. When others ask how I've come to be here, the answer I recite is gleaned from overheard conversations and newspaper clippings. There is no hard evidence that I was ever in Laos or Thailand, except for the photographs.

The earliest photograph in my album is a billfold-sized black and white from Thailand—my VISA photo. I am four years old and staring straight at the camera with a mesmerized look. The VISA would be used for entrance into America, or Australia, whichever opportunity came first.

When I look at this photograph, I am reminded of every single photo from Thailand that has long since been lost. The individual frames of my father and mother, lanky and tired of waiting, wearing the only clothes they owned. Their faces expressionless as they held small slate boards in front of them on which their names and birth dates were written in English. That slate board could just as well have held a number and an assignment to a life-term cell exiled from the country they called home. There's a black-and-white photo of my grandmother—the only one ever taken of her—at a photographer's booth in Vientiane. My uncle and older brother flank either side of her like guards. She sits on a bamboo wing chair like a matron presiding. Our only color photograph taken in Thailand has my grandfather, my parents, my uncle and his wife, me, and my new brother standing in a row. They're all gone now, those images—except that I remember them. Had I known they would disappear, I would have pulled them and buried them.

Next in my album is my family in Vermont at the School for International Training. Here there is snow. There are my parents. And there is me and my brother, and there is Naoko—one of our teachers—behind us, holding my hand up for a wave hello. My mother is lugging a tote with books. We are all wearing wool coats. I know that when my mother boarded that plane in Thailand, she did not know there were places in the world where there was no green, where the trees looked dead, where the wind was mean, and it felt like you were falling off the world into a space which existed between lands of welcome. My parents were leaving the refugee camps where Mom walked the streets selling what she'd foraged—mushrooms I think, and where Dad worked somewhere, but I don't know where because he never talked about anything outside of America. I know they were leaving any hope of returning, of working their oxen, of blessing my grandmother when she died, and of reuniting with their first-born son whom they'd left behind in Grandma's care.

I think about how being human hurts so much and about why leaving places we love hurts so much, and that promises don't keep. I think that if Grandma hadn't held onto my brother so tightly, hadn't loved him so much, hadn't pledged all her love and all her days to him that I would have never felt the great weight of his absence in the fifteen years that I didn't know him. I also think that if my parents hadn't loved her and respected her so much, that if they hadn't reasoned and talked themselves into their escape, neither my brother nor I would have resented it. He wouldn't have hated them.

He wouldn't have caught mice and birds or roasted them to eat. He wouldn't have caught flying insects to fry after Grandma died because no one else had stepped up to take care of an orphaned nine-year-old boy whose parents, he thought, had left him for good.

I think about my mother, who simply wants to go back and make peace with the ghosts of her past that are probably still wandering around out there lost among the rice paddies and riverboats because she hasn't honored them enough, and she hasn't given them a safe place to go. I remember all of her talk about her animals and the night we left, with the wind blowing through the abandoned house. I think about the wind howling down the valley, knocking over our empty bowls and steamers, with its hands through the tall rice like a lover's caress as if the stalks would talk and tell it which path we took.

I picture me in a sling, tied closely to her breast, of them, my age now, running, the soldiers on night guard pacing the foot paths of the mountains bordering Thailand. I think about how trained they were—just like my father was trained because he was one of them once—but he doesn't want to be anymore, and that's why we were running. The Red Army wouldn't take him away. They wouldn't take his family away. They wouldn't take his life's hope away. The Viets and Americans would bring bombs to his country in the war, but he didn't know this. That wasn't why we snuck out in the cover of night really.

My friend Connie told me about a Cambodian man who has a metal plate in his head from a gunshot somewhere in the dark mountains he was crossing.

"Brave," Connie said. "So brave."

What's worse than a metal plate? My father could have lost a leg like Phan's father did, who walked with a crutch at thirty-seven. Or worse, he could have been shot down during the full moon when one of the comrades spotted our silhouettes slinking through the jungle. We all could have died that way—left for the morning sun. No dog tags. No wallets with our pictures or papers. No asylum.

I think about my father who will not talk about all that's left to my imagination—not the way other fathers do. He won't express what is bottled up inside, not like Oi's father, who's painted five large pictures on poster paper of what he misses: stilt houses, brown and dried out, rice paddies and oxen—the animal for which I'm named. He's given a place for the rivers and steamy mountains still stirring within him. They're no great art; they're not framed preciously and stored away. His pictures are tacked to a wall in the sitting room, one to another in a panoramic assemblage. They serve as portals to what he'd left behind. Oi's father also sings about it in his bamboo mouth organ. His wife writes letters disguised as ballads, and she wails to his tunes. They are about snow, about October leaves, about family ghosts, and the heavy-hot monsoon. I think they've found peace where my Dad hasn't.

My father has no windows to look through, no panorama of memory to ground him. He's been to the psychologist since I was sixteen, but I didn't know it—and he didn't tell me. My Dad, the one so close to my life, the one, who had he not have been a soldier once, wouldn't have been able to pass us through the dark shadow of danger which stood between our Laos burning up and the temporary sanctuary of Thai refugee camps. I wish I'd known then, been different; I would have understood then.

I read transcripts of his sessions found in an expanding file tucked far in a cabinet of other unrelated things. I read and read and could not stop reading. I did not care that his nightmares were his secret and that he'd rather give them to strangers and not to me. I wanted them. I walked inside and became them. The enemies in fatigues in the dark. On the blackest night, he could still see their uniforms, and in the dark he died every time. I don't care. Even still, his secrets should have been mine, too.

I think about how hard it is to leave, and I think about the night he kicked me out of my home and the expectations he'd put me up against. He said that I should marry or study or work if I wanted house and food and love. He told me he loved me that night. It was the first time I'd heard it. I was seventeen, and I knew I'd never hear it again. I cried in my soup. I crawled back into bed, and I cried. Mom crawled in with me because she knew how much it hurt to be torn away from home. She put her arm around my shoulder, which she'd never done before or since—except in a newspaper photograph—and she sat there with me while I cried. Her tears soon joined mine. She never told me she loved me, but she told me this secret: my father was a tormented man.

His nightmares haunted him night and day. He quit work because the anxiety was too great, and he beat her. Not physically, but with his words. He told her how he hated her. He wanted her to move out—leave him alone—that he didn't want a wife anymore. I barely listened; I didn't want her sorrow on top of my own. My heart was pounding in my ears; my tears would not stop. I did not want to leave.

I think about leaving and loving people and about how much work life is. I understand now that when my brother came to the States and loathed our parents for his abandonment, my father's shame was brought to the surface. My brother was a reminder of a past that wouldn't erase. He represented the night that changed all our lives, and my father's primary role in that episode. He represented our ties to the homeland and this complex relationship with Americans whose destruction brought forth this change of events, but among whom he lives and tolerates, and my father can't reconcile that.

I think about love. I know that I love America because I am American. I dream American dreams. I know also that I love my rich past because I don't remember it. I don't relive the escape every night in my dreams because I was a baby then, and I've become comfortable with the distance. The story is more like a myth than a memory. How could I possibly be comfortable with this distance? I think about passion, and I think about being split open by love and torment and about the refreshing feel of flesh tearing in two. I don't love this distance. I don't love it. I want to be torn apart like my parents were. I want to molt out of my old shell into someone new, somewhere else. I want to feel the cool of the spring wind against that moist new skin. I want to smell hope blowing across the plains of independence and yearning, just as my parents must have when they climbed the steel steps of the airplane and left home for good.

PHAYVANH LUEKHAMHAN's writing has been featured in many public readings, art exhibits, and on the radio. They are for sale on the streets of Vermont and have traveled as far as the Federated States of Micronesia.

Flowering

To Drew

i

I walk out on the fourteenth-story balcony.
The air is cold, the lake opaque
Except for the waves, hesitant, this morning,
Fretting toward the shrinking shore.

Hands on the rail, I look down,
Turn to see a band of birds fly below
Toward the copse of skyscrapers, stoning the sky.

ii

Once, a few years ago, I walked hand in hand
With my grandson down the small-town
Sidewalk back from town.
I don't know how far we were
From his home, but
He stopped suddenly and looked up at me,

"Nana," he asked, "What does it mean to be brave?"

iii

We may have been talking about flowers—
The crocus or daffodils—the first
To break through the hard soil of winter,
The ones who can't stand to wait
For the safety of spring,
The hard-headed ones who long to see
What's above the tonnage of crusted earth
Weighted with icy crystals,

The tough-minded and the ones more curious
Than their fear of being crushed or frozen
Sharp as a crystal, and
The ones who carp and the ones who whistle
Themselves through the iceberg ceiling
Of their underground villages
To sate something in their hungering souls.
We might have been talking about crocus.

iv

"To be brave means . . ." I hesitated . . .
"You're not afraid . . . ," he finished, as he twisted
His face into a hard knot and fashioned
His four-year-old body into a martial pose,
"And you don't cry and run away.
You stay even when you're afraid."

v

When he returned from his frozen pose, he looked
Straight as the sun into my eyes, and asked,
"Can you make my brother braver? Can you . . ?"

vi

It's still winter here, the waves slowing to flat stillness
As I look past the memory of his face:
That deeply held thought cracks open,
        rising out of the icy mudhive—
        The dreambowl of his mind—
With the hard-headedness of a quickening love
To rise above the frozen surface and begin
The work of melting . . . the earth . . .

SARAH A. ODISHOO, a professor of English at Columbia College in Chicago, has been published in *New Letters*, *Confrontations*, *River Teeth*, *Laurel Review*, *Aura Literary Arts Review*, *Berkeley Fiction Review*, *Florida Review*, *Fugue*, *Georgetown Review*, *Jeopardy Magazine*, *Left Curve*, *Libido*, *Limestone*, *Lynx Eye*, *Pikeville Review*, *Portland Review*, and *RiverSedge*. She was nominated for the Pushcart Prize in Short Stories (1997) and has been a finalist in competitions, such as the Nelson Algren Short Fiction Competition, Nimrod Poetry Contest, and the Saint Agnes Eve Poetry Contest.

CHRISTINE KALLSTROM

The Wild Corner

WHEN WE MOVED INTO OUR FIRST HOME, I forged a circular trail in a wild corner of the backyard to represent a pathway to God. This mini-journey was to remind walkers when they arrived back at the beginning of the trail that God had been with them all along. I wanted them to know that *God is where we are.*

Forty years later, that corner of the yard is still wild. At times when I sit on the porch looking out at the wildness, I remember journeys of my lifetime—each filled with enormous energy and enthusiasm for the unknown and for the ongoing search for more insight.

The earliest journeys I recall were the Sunday afternoons my parents would take my little sister and me to grandmother's house. Aunts, uncles, cousins, and other kin greeted us, each so different. Some swooped us up high in the air, rubbed us with scratchy whiskers, tapped us on the head, tickled us, hugged us tightly against the firmness of corset stays, or suffocated us in the aroma of perfume or cigar smoke. Each person—in their own way—made me feel that I was an important part of the family gathering, just by being there.

Books were another source of passages into destinations both real and fantasized, each impregnating my imagination in a way that would morph time and shape my encounters with reality. There were the woods where Snow White was abandoned and Bambi's mother was shot. There were stories of poverty and evil people or of children getting lost to be captured by pirates or wicked witches.

Surprisingly, I recall few spiritual journeys at a very young age. Everything about Jesus and God and the Holy Spirit (yes—they were separately identified back then as three persons) was a known—a status quo—not to be pondered or doubted but a fixed part of my upbringing. Just recite the creeds, pray the prayers, sip the communion, sing the hymns, pass the plate, and all was well in this world.

As an adult, my spiritual journey encompassed being an organist, choir director, a children's choir clinician, serving on national hymnal committees, and writing Sunday school curricula. My journey up to that time might have been subtitled: *As It Was in the Beginning, Is Now and Ever Shall Be. Amen.* It was all a "done deal," done by those before me, like a well-trodden, back-and-forth path, with no unknown turns.

While I might have been eternally encapsulated into a frozen faith, reinforced by all the knowns of my lifetime, an event of catastrophic consequence changed my life, tearing down the fixed fortresses of my faith. Coming home late one evening from my chairperson duties, I found my front door locked. I was greeted by my distressed husband who had taken our three children to his mother's house. He gave me an ultimatum—be his wife and the mother of our children or spend all my time working for the church.

I decided to follow a new path—one that would enable me to be home with the children as well as make our marriage a priority over playing music for the women's missionary society, weddings, church services, or flying off to hymnal meetings and workshops. The next morning, I went bawling along a new path to a nearby university, where I began the first of three degrees, six teaching certifications, and an introduction to a world outside the box that had defined my life. I reminded myself *God is with us where we are.*

In being divested of my lifelong props of rituals, hymns, prayers, and biblical scriptures, I had to start from scratch. It was through this new journey that transformation would begin. I had to see the life journey through new eyes.

Another dimension to this new passage occurred on Palm Sunday, 1969. Our fourth child was born, eighteen years after the birth of his older brother. By this time, my coursework readings had introduced me to the writings of Comenius, Pestalozzi, Rousseau, Froebel, Steiner, Montessori, Bruner, McLuhan, Gardner, and others who wrote about the development of the inner child. I realized for the first time how profoundly the sights, sounds, and movements of the world were impacting the internal responses of our youngest son. As we looked at the world anew through his eyes, we discovered how critical our interactions were and how our words to his experiences would be planted firmly in his mind for a lifetime.

Observing our youngest child changed our thinking and lives. In 1996, we decided to create a new kind of parent–professional cooperative on the grounds of American Airlines DFW campus. The school's mission was "to enable normal, gifted, and handicapped children to climb to the heights that are their own." Rather than traditional, sit-down, "be still" instruction, the school was propaedeutic in nature, including both traditional studies and the creative arts, augmented with nature studies and travel to England, Switzerland, Central America, and other parts of the world. A campus in the Davy Crockett National Forest was added in 1989 to provide environmental education. We called it "Treetops-in-the-Forest."

CHANGE led to new perspectives. I thought about the gatherings at my grandmother's house and wondered about the roots of such a motley crew of kinfolk. I learned that my great-grandparents came to America from France and Switzerland as part of a Utopian colony founded by a French philosopher Charles Fourier who believed that both men and women should be free to follow the passions of their lives. The colony LaReunion was on the outskirts of Dallas in the mid-1800s and was filled with artists, musicians, tailors, physicians, boot makers, astronomers, vintners, and naturalists. I imagined their nightly gatherings as similar to my childhood family gatherings.

This ongoing transformation made me see my husband in a new light. He taught economics and history in high school, but his deeper love was nature. After serving as a Marine in World War II, he no longer wanted to hunt to kill animals. Instead he tracked animals deep into the woods to photograph them. It was this appreciation of nature that gave him the great joy of taking children on outdoor hikes and teaching them how to observe and care for all living things.

One of the most amazing parts of my journey has been leaving behind all the ritualistic rigidities of my past. I discovered the teachings of Emanuel Swedenborg in which I was drawn into a constant awareness of God's presence and purposes in my life. Swedenborg wrote about uses, that every living thing has a use and purpose. As our "uses" become known to us, each day greets us with opportunities to put those uses into practice, wherever we are and whatever we can do to impact the world around us.

Looking out at that wild corner, I still believe wholeheartedly that *God is where we are*. I am keenly aware that we awaken each day to be alive to the uses God has for us on all our journeys, along new paths and old, filled with meanings through all the moments and patterns and sequences that unfold in our lives as our transformation is completing itself.

CHRISTINE KALLSTROM holds a doctorate in early childhood education and a master's degree in special education. She has six TEA teaching credentials, most recently completing a graduate environmental education course. She has taught at public and independent schools, including the University of North Texas and Texas Wesleyan.

I Think of My Grandfather

on a cramped ship
headed toward Ellis Island.
Fog, fog horns for a
lullaby. The black
pines, a frozen pear.
Straw roofs on fire.
If there were postcards
from the sea there might
have been a Dear
Hannah or Mama, hand
colored with salt.
I will come and get you.
If the branches are
green, pick the apples.
When I write next, I will
have a pack on my
back, string and tin.
I dream about the snow
in the mountains. I never
liked it but I dream of
you tying a scarf
around my hair, your
words that white dust

LYN LIFSHIN has published more than a hundred books of poetry, including *Before It's Light* (1999–2000), winner of the Paterson Poetry Award; *Cold Comfort* (1997); *Another Woman Who Looks Like Me* (2005); and *A New Film about a Woman in Love with the Dead*. Her newest book is about the short-lived race horse, Ruffian. *The Licorice Daughter: My Year with Ruffian*. Soon to be published by Arielle Press *Poets (Mostly) Who Have Touched Me, Living and Dead. All True, Especially the Lies* (2006).

In Brooklyn

Henri Matisse.
Le jeune marin
[Sailor Boy].
Graphite on paper,
10 x 7¼ in.,
1906. Art Gallery
of Ontario, Toronto.
Gift of Sam and Ayala
Zacks, 1970.
Photograph AGO/
Sean Weaver.

IN BROOKLYN A BOY was measured by the distance in sewer plates he could hit a rubber ball, and only his very closest friend called him by his first name, and the saddest of sights was to see a building rising where once there had been a vacant lot.

To a boy in Brooklyn, too, the least esteemed of all things on earth was a girl. Frankie Keating believed sincerely that girls deserved the low regard in which they were held because, besides being crybabies and having little idea of what was fun, they were sneaky, two-faced, and squealers, except for a few, like Elissa Mancini, who was as regular as any guy, and Isobel Sheerin who . . . well, that was one of the things about the whole business of girls that Frankie didn't understand at all.

First of all, despite the fact that every boy on Schaeffer Street would say he hated girls, each of them had a girlfriend. It did not mean the boy showed the least sign of interest in the girl or even ever spoke to her. In fact, likely neither of them had much to do with the choice. But some law dictated that every boy have a girl assigned to him and in some inscrutable way a pairing was decided and universally recognized. Why the system should exist, and how it could be active in the face of the general attitude towards girls, was beyond Frankie's comprehension.

Secondly, no matter how much other girls gave him a pain in the neck, however contrary it was to the way other guys felt, because none of them ever showed any sign of liking their appointed girls, Frankie knew that truly and with all his heart he liked Isobel Sheerin. He could make no sense out of it; he did not try. All he knew was that whenever he saw Isobel, or thought of her, with her skinny legs and blue dresses and a nose that was pointed and tiny, like a bird's beak really, but pretty, he was eaten up with longing for her.

Elissa Mancini was olive-skinned and had eyes like black agates and of all the kids on Schaeffer Street Frankie wished his personality was most like hers. Elissa was full of good spirits and open in every way and she never put on airs. When Elissa liked you she liked you without reservation, and she was as trustworthy as Lloyd himself. Frankie felt everyone in the world should be like Elissa. But it was Isobel he liked in a singular way, with her dainty walk and pointed nose and shades of blue.

Elissa called now to Frankie and Lloyd Keller, his best friend, as they came by her stoop before any others of the gang were in sight. She stood at the top of the steps with Isobel. Frankie would not look at Isobel, but he was aware she was wearing a crisply fresh dress with blue and white checks, and he could not help the tension she caused.

"Would you like to come over to my aunt's house on Decatur Street tonight?" Elissa said. "We can play Monopoly in the backyard and have soda and cookies. Just you two and Isobel and me."

In Brooklyn the early summer evenings, when it was cool and still light and the day was not yet done, were the most wonderful times of all. Baths had been taken after a hard day's play and newly laundered "good" clothes replaced play clothes. A boy relished the ring-a-leav-io soon to be played, and later maybe, when it was dark, there would be a gathering on a stoop and a game of Truth, Dare or Consequences (in which, in another of the anomalies of custom, girls were permitted to participate). A boy, too, in the leisure before activities began, might indulge his dreams of playing for the Dodgers, or going on safari, or becoming a millionaire and building for all the kids baseball diamonds and curbs reserved for playing marbles, and none of the aspirations seemed unreasonable. He sensed the wonder of existence and all the world had to offer.

But never in all the summer evenings on Schaeffer Street had there been a prospect like the one now presented to Frankie. His bottled-up yearning for Isobel burst forth and swept him up in a torrent of desire to be with her in a little company of four under the arbor in Elissa's aunt's yard on Decatur Street.

Only . . .

Unbelievably . . .

Lloyd said to Elissa, "Nah! We got other things to do."

Frankie looked at Lloyd as if the words were incomprehensible.

"Come on," Elisa urged. "We'll have a nice time."

"Nah," Lloyd repeated. "We're going with the guys."

With the guys? To do what? Frankie raged. They had no special plans. And if they did, who cared about them? An evening with Isobel in privacy? More delighting joy was unimaginable. There'd be talk later, of course, but it did not concern him. Yet, as Lloyd moved on, Frankie fell in step. Even, incredibly, he said to Elissa:

"Yeah. We gotta go."

Frankie was certain he saw a flicker of disappointment in Elissa's Italian eyes. He felt he was wrapped like a mummy and wanted fiercely to burst the bandages and make Lloyd understand *he* wanted to go with Elissa and Isobel. But a force restrained him. He did not try to argue. Merely he strode along in silent fury, until, a way down the block, he blurted:

"Why didn't you want to go with them, Lloyd?"

Lloyd looked at him in astonishment. "You wanted to?"

Frankie held back for an instant, then spouted with a vehemence that laid open his anger, "*Yes!* I wanted to."

Lloyd stared. He said nothing, as if he were pondering a facet of his friend he had never seen before.

The two boys saw the gang gathered near the Irving Avenue corner.

"Oh, boy! Ring-a-leavio!" Lloyd said in anticipation.

It was Frankie's favorite evening-time game too, but instead of joining in savoring the prospect, he said to Lloyd:

"I gotta go. I just remembered I got something to do."

Lloyd looked at him in bafflement. Frankie hurried on ahead, past the knot of boys near the corner, hardly acknowledging them, and turned on Irving Avenue toward Decatur. It was a peculiar thing for him to do in the eyes of the gang because none of them had any business that way. Out of their sight Frankie ran hard, up on his toes as he had heard champion sprinters did. The rest of the gang might not care about their girls, he asserted, but he was different. To circle the whole block and return to Elissa's stoop was a necessity. She and Isobel might no longer be there but he had to try. It was an affirmation that had to be made. Just before the turn into the opposite end of Schaeffer Street, he stopped running.

His walk, as he caught his breath, was grim. He could not see the girls when he was ten houses from Elissa's but they could be sitting on the doorstep hidden from view. He tried to appear not to be in a hurry, indeed to seem that he had no specific destination at all. It made no difference: when he came close enough he saw that Elissa and Isobel were gone.

He walked more and more slowly, staring at the red-painted stone steps as he passed, hoping still that in some way the girls were there, but the stoop and the doorway were deserted.

He thought now not of the mission to get to the stoop, but of the object. The sense of loss came upon him. It was as if, after all his longing, he could have had possession of Isobel, though he had no idea what possession might mean, and she had been ripped away from him. It hurt, truly and physically, and the nature of denied desire was so incomprehensible that, although boys in Brooklyn never cried, Frankie wanted to cry.

He saw Isobel in his mind, in the blue-and-white checked dress, laughing with Elissa and buying up property in Monopoly and, maybe, talking about him. Elissa's aunt would be bringing refreshments. But it was only Isobel he missed, and all he felt as he walked beyond Elissa's house was the misery and agony of deprivation.

Mechanically, he headed back to the gang. He became aware of the buildings and alleys of Schaeffer Street, and the wall of an apartment house where kingball was played, and a potsy court drawn on the sidewalk by the girls, but none of these came into focus. All of existence was remote. There was hardly thought even, until, out of a surging within him, Frankie said, almost aloud:

"I don't care about the rest of them. I like Isobel."

Saying it was the beginning of release. He took note of the score of a racket-ball game chalked on the asphalt. He glanced into the finished basement of the only single-family house on the block. Ache began to ease. For a moment he felt a kind of meanness, then a calm. The great protector of the young, the ability to forget, drew its mantle over him.

Minutes later the fastest and trickiest ring-a-leavio player on Schaeffer Street was speeding down an alley headed for the garages behind the houses, oblivious of the arbor in a certain backyard, and unaware of the existence of Isobel Sheerin and skinny legs and a tiny nose and the color blue.

But on another summer evening, when all of the Schaeffer Street gang were at a birthday party and, though girls were never considered part of the gang, they were extended for the occasion temporary privilege of lower-grade membership, an extraordinary game called Post Office had been initiated, and Frankie found himself summoned to a bedroom where Isobel Sheerin waited for him.

He came into the dimly lit room, his heart accelerating. He made himself tough, to conceal his apprehension, but there was only tenderness in his disposition. It stunned him to see Isobel standing alone, only for him, skinny and extravagantly pretty in a blue satin dress. She averted her eyes, not in rejection of him, only in modesty.

He came close to her, slightly taller than she. He would have to bend to kiss her. To kiss Isobel.

He was intoxicated with the anticipation of it. It did not bother him that he did not know which way to tilt his head. At the last moment she looked at him, silent still. The pink of her face was excruciating, and the tiny nose, and her scent was fresh and flower-like and totally beyond his experience.

He touched with his lips *hers,* they were thin and cool and still, for only an instant. Thrill coursed in him. He was electrified. In a fleeting millisecond he sensed Paradise. There was unlocked to him for evermore, although he did not know it, entrance to the supreme area of life.

That was what it was, to kiss Isobel Sheerin, who wore a shiny blue dress and was quiet and birdlike and only for him, in a party game in Brooklyn when he was eleven.

Brought up in Brooklyn, CHARLES CHERRY served on a submarine in WWII before going on to Yale and Columbia. His output of fiction, articles, and longer nonfiction has been mixed with a business career that took him to many countries in Europe, Africa, and Asia. He lives now in Florida, where he is at work on his fourth novel.

Whiteheart

1.
That winter we stopped sharing a bed.
The sex had become perfunctory.
Even the sleep was bad as we
turned and pulled against each other,
covers stolen back and forth.
A gust of boxes and suitcases and then quiet.
From behind the living room window
I watched her loaded car drive away.

2.
The evenings were dark so early,
I wrapped up in one of my five new
pairs of flannel pajamas;
pushed jigsaw pieces around a table—
an Early American, New England snow scene.
Horse-drawn sleds carrying
logs and jugs of maple syrup.
Sharp-steepled grey churches.
I took a month to finish it.

Then I moved on to my computer screen.
I stumbled on webcams—
cameras trained for twenty-four hours a day
on people having sex and dusting houseplants;
or places like Times Square and the
Little White Chapel in Las Vegas.
On animals—the shark cam, the puppy cam.
The bear cam. I tried that one.

Whiteheart was a two-year-old black bear.
She was hibernating. She was pregnant.
The bear scientist hoped
she would give birth in the spring.

I checked in daily.
I had always imagined
that bear dens looked like
the vast, roomy caves of storybooks.
This was little more than a burrowed hole,
the infrared camera hidden in its small opening.
Whiteheart's head was visible,
just a patch of dark fur

surrounded by snow.
Sometimes she shifted
in her long, undisturbed sleep.
Other times, I could hardly tell
if she moved at all.

One day I realized that
I was watching *a bear hibernate.*
Even the Vegas wedding cam would be
better than this, I thought.

The days lengthened.
I walked through my neighborhood
in the early evenings,
thought about planting a garden.

Occasionally, I still checked on Whiteheart.
The bear scientist said she was fine
until the day he said she wasn't.
There was no picture on the screen,
just a report that she had miscarried,
pulled her radio collar off and left.

She was somewhere in the Minnesota woods.
The scientist was going to look for her
and set up another cam.
He was hopeful that
there would be more cubs.
She was young.
Bears can live a long time.

Born in Mobile, Alabama, CHARLOTTE MCCAFFREY moved to California after two decades in the Midwest. Her work has appeared or is forthcoming
in *The Comstock Review, Confrontation, Hampden-Sydney Poetry Review,
Madison Review, Phoebe, Poetry International, Porcupine Magazine,
Sojourner, Sulphur River Literary Review, Women's Studies Quarterly,* and
others. She teaches a special education class in the San Francisco Bay area.

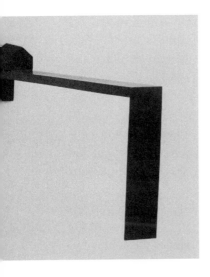

Give It Up

ALL MY LIFE I HAVE BEEN PART OF THE PRESBYTERIAN CHURCH. When I was a child, I attended Sunday school, church camps, and family retreats. As a teenager, the idea of radically following Jesus and becoming a "Jesus freak" was not very appealing, but I strived to live a life of love and peace. Giving up my life for God seemed attainable, especially since I didn't seem to possess much at that age. But as I got older, with more responsibilities—a husband, children, and more possessions—I looked again at what it might mean to save my life by losing it, as Jesus suggested. I certainly didn't want to literally give up my life; I even had thoughts and fears that if I prayed, "God, I surrender, I give up my way for your way," I might have to do something I really didn't want to do at all, perhaps even leave my family and become a missionary or something. My perplexity seems silly now, but it was real to me then.

As an adult, I've thought a lot about "giving up" my way for another, my position, so to speak, as a way of actually transforming my relationships and my life in the way that the divine does so graciously for us. Like every couple my husband David and I have had many disagreements. We generally resolve them quickly, but there are those times when a quick resolution is nowhere in sight. One such time, one evening at bedtime, we both got angry and upset. Over what, I don't exactly remember. He strongly felt he was right, and, of course, I *knew* I was right. There we lay in the darkness, and between us there was that cold, heavy silence. He said, "I can't sleep; I'm going out to the living room to read."

I thought to myself, "Fine." I also thought to myself, the best thing to do would be to apologize for getting angry. But I just couldn't seem to make myself move or speak out. After all, I was right, and he was wrong. I realized I'd have to talk myself through it because being in this angry state of mind, I definitely did not want to give up my way for another more loving way. I wanted to hold on tightly because he was the one who should apologize first. I could see this was clearly not working. I prayed for guidance and received strength. I began to

Joel Shapiro. *Untitled (House on Shelf).* Bronze, 12⅞ x 2½ x 18½ in., 1974. Museum of Modern Art, New York, New York. Artists Rights Society, New York. Digital Image © The Museum of Modern Art / Licensed by SCALA / Art Resource, New York. © Joel Shapiro / Artists Rights Society (ARS), New York.

talk myself through it: sit up, put my feet on the floor, and walk to the living room (all the while not wanting to go). As I came to where David was sitting, I reached out my hand, touched his shoulder, and said, "I'm sorry."

It was as if a wave of calm, of generosity, of love, came over me in that instant. Not just an emotion, but a physical sensation. I certainly didn't expect this incredible feeling. Our anger and pride melted away, transforming the two of us. We each gave up believing that our individual way was right and that the other's was wrong, thus restoring our love.

What do we stand to lose from "giving up" or "surrendering"? Is it that we really lose our power, our control, and our strength? Or could it be just the opposite? I believe when we have the courage to surrender, we gain compassion, generosity, and love. When I did finally choose to give up my will for God's will and pray for guidance, instead of feeling "not in control" or uncertain, I felt *totally free,* no resistance, a peacefulness, like coming home to God's unconditional love. I could sense challenges ahead of me, but I was excited, not anxious or fearful.

One of my greatest lessons in unconditional love and acceptance occurred with my mother when I was a student in Ohio. During my second year of college, I had something serious to say to my parents. I had put it off for as long as I could, but I knew I'd eventually need to ask for their help, guidance, and forgiveness. When I finally called, my mother answered. I told her I wanted to come home.

Puzzled, she asked, "Why?"

I said, "I just want to come home."

There was a pause, and then she asked, with a mother's intuition, "Are you pregnant?"

I couldn't even get the words out of my mouth. There was a very long silence. Then I broke down and cried, "Yes."

Of course, I'd been afraid that she'd be angry and disappointed in me for being thoughtless and irresponsible. But without anger, without judgment, and without hesitation, my mother said to me, "Oh, honey, you just get on that first plane, and you come on home." At that moment, her forgiveness and her unconditional love transformed my fear and my uncertainty. In that moment, I was already home.

JENNIFER PASTON SPEARS received her undergraduate degree from Louisiana State University while raising her first-born child, Jessica, followed by marriage and two more children. Jennifer has a ceramic jewelry business and regularly participates in coursework offered by Landmark Education Corporation.

Rachel Sleeps Over

Jean Auguste
Dominique Ingres.
*Portrait of Marie
Marcotte at the Age
of Sixteen Months.*
Graphite, 9⅝ x 7½ in.,
1830. Yale University Art
Gallery, New Haven,
Connecticut.
Bequest of
Edith Malvina K.
Wetmore.

THIS TIME SHE SAYS SHE IS GOING TO STAY THE WHOLE NIGHT. She's had plenty of sleepovers, but always accompanied by her two big brothers. Rachel once tried to stay at our house without her brothers but wept copious tears and wailed. To the rescue came her Mama.

This night she is going to sleep in the secret bed, a sofa in the alcove adjoining our bedroom, which, with the pillows and bolsters removed, transforms magically into a bed.

All goes well. She watches television until she is very tired, and with her special blanket our granddaughter falls asleep.

My husband and I congratulate each other and prepare for a good night's rest. At precisely the stroke of midnight, Rachel turns into a raging pumpkin and screams. "Stessy, Stessy. I need to go home. Now! Call my mother. Now. Tell her to come get me. Now."

I realize this is no nightmare, shake myself, and trot into the alcove. "What's the matter, dear? Are you having a bad dream?"

She does not answer. "Call my mother! Now!" she yells. "Right now! I need to sleep in my own bed!"

"Let's talk," I say, and carry her to my bed. "Charlie," I say to my poor sleeping spouse, "go sleep in the secret bed."

He stumbles out of our bed and cozies into hers, only to return a few minutes later. "Here," he mumbles, holding his arm out, on which is draped the sacrosanct blanky.

Rachel and I negotiate from midnight to 2:30. I give her the sleeping teddy, a present I had bought with this crisis in mind. "She'll help you sleep," I promise. "She's magic."

Rachel closes her eyes. "No," she says, her eyes wide open again. "It's not working."

"How about if we cuddle, and I hold you and tell you stories? It's almost morning. You don't want Mommy to drive in the dark. Okay?"

"Okay."

So I hold and cuddle and murmur made-up stories until she reluctantly drops off, but any time I let go of her, she stirs and says, "Don't let go." At 5:30 her eyes pop open. "It's morning. Call Mommy."

"AH, RACHEL," I SAY. "Let's go down and have a cup of coffee."

She looks at her ignorant grandmother and rebukes me. "I'm not allowed to have caffeinated beverages," she says. "Sometimes I can have decaffeinated tea. Call my mother. Now."

"Rachel," I say, "I need a favor. I'd like to watch cartoons, and I'd like company. Would you watch a little with me?"

Her face lights up. "Okay," she says. I say a silent prayer of thanks to the cartoon network. We watch, and I drink a lot of very strong, very caffeinated coffee. We last until 9:00. I dial her mother, and put Rachel on the phone.

"Mommy, I stayed the whole night. I'm very proud of myself." She says, "I slept in the secret bed, and a little with Stessy. Now come and get me."

We go upstairs to get washed and dressed. We work on puzzles until her daddy comes.

"Go home," she tells him. "I'm having a play date with Stessy."

"Ix-nay," I say to her father, who explains that her mother misses her and takes her home. She gives me a high five as a final congratulatory acknowledgement, and off she goes, pink suitcase in hand.

I fall into bed. My husband later informs me that my snores could be heard in Eastchester, the next town, and perhaps even in Yonkers.

STEPHANIE KAPLAN COHEN and her husband live and work in Westchester County, New York. They are the parents of three grown children, and eight grandchildren, all of whom are exceptional in all ways.

ROBERT BLY

The Old Fishing Lines

Sometimes I get in my car on a late October day
And drive north. Everything that I haven't done—
Raking, visiting—all those reasons for not living—
Fall away. I pass half-abandoned summer towns,
Admiring the shadows thrown by bare trees
On bare lakes where cold waves lap the sand.

The renegade minister—the one they all gossip
About—would see those waves too, after throwing
His Sunday hat out the window. He'll be
All right. Death hugs the underside of oak leaves.
In each cove you pass you will see
What you had to say no to once.

It's all right if you walk down to the shore.
You'll feel time passing, the way the summer has.
You'll see the little holes that raindrops leave in fine sand,
And those old fishing lines driven up on the rocks.

ROBERT BLY's two most recent books are *The Night Abraham Called to the Stars* and *My Sentence Was a Thousand Years of Joy*. Both books are made up of ghazals (a compact poetic form well-known in Islamic culture, orginating in tenth-century Persia). He has been translating Hafez in recent years with the help of Leonard Lewisohn. The most recent issue of his magazine is called *The Thousands #1*.

Will You Be a Priest?

I HATE YOUR CAR, Margaret pronounced angrily. She stood in my bedroom doorway looking formidable in her nightshirt and mammoth high-top sneakers.

"What are you talking about?" I asked, surprised by her outburst so early in the morning. "My car has nothing to do with it. You're going to school. It'll be okay."But I knew my daughter wasn't finished.

"That car sucks. I wish I lived with Daddy," she said stomping off.

We weren't talking about cars. My thirteen-year-old daughter had voiced both our misgivings about starting the school year—middle school for her and my teaching at San Diego High School.

I sat on the side of my bed to put on my teaching shoes. The black leather flats seemed like the heavy boots of a mountain climber. When I stood and looked in the mirror, a forty-year-old single mother looked back. Could I face another year of high-school students, theater productions, and the crabby man in the supply room? I admitted to myself in the mirror I wanted to leave teaching and go to graduate school to seek a spiritual center, perhaps even find God.

In the kitchen I made tea. Daisy, my golden spaniel, gazed up at me. She looked downhearted, as if she knew how I felt. "Cheer up, old girl," I said. A burst of Margaret's fury emanated from her bedroom. Was she shoving furniture? "Take care of Margaret," I added.

WHEN I PULLED OFF THE RAMP ONTO THE FREEWAY, my rusty, old Ambassador stalled. "Rats," I said to Steve, the teenager who rode with me to school. "I'm so sorry."

Opposite:
Barbara Hepworth.
Two Figures.
Polished wood and white painted teak, 57 x 35⅞ x 17½ in., 1954–1955. The Art Institute of Chicago. Bequest of Solomon B. Smith (1985.1278). Photography © The Art Institute of Chicago.

"Doesn't matter," he grinned. Steve had freckles and the easy-going nature of a bespectacled Huck Finn. "Good excuse to be late."

"I take this as a sign from God," I sighed.

"You got it." He stretched his arms above his head and leaned back.

That's the morning I decided to leave teaching and go to Berkeley to study religion. Who knows what moves us to change? For me, it was the shoes, the dog's face, and the breakdown of my car. The signs were calling me to obey a desire that had intensified to an obsession: I wanted to study theology and make a search for God. I'd take my daughter and our dog. Maybe Margaret would grow out of her defiance in the quiet of a college town away from her friends and the temptations of urban life.

At the end of that school year, I hosted a cast party to celebrate the successful run of our student production *Up the Down Staircase*. I knew I had to tell my drama class I was leaving teaching. My reasons were not romantic—like taking off with a lover—and I wanted them to understand.

Fourteen teenagers hurried into the living room, bringing a burst of noise. I can't tell them, I thought, but as soon as we'd served ourselves, I announced to the diners scattered over the room, "Some of you may have heard I'm leaving." Steve squinted at me, suspicious. I continued, "I'm going to Berkeley to study religion . . . I'll never forget you." I cleared my throat, glancing into the darkened kitchen.

"Will you be a priest?" asked José.

"Catholic priest? Oh, José, maybe I'll be the first lady priest. Who knows?"

AT THAT TIME OUR AMERICAN CULTURE SEEMED DIVIDED over religious matters. We had the Death of God, the conviction that God must not exist after the horrors of the world wars, a war in Korea, and a protracted bloodbath in Vietnam. Then, there were the people who were leaving organized religion and seeking comfort in what they called spirituality as expressed in Eastern philosophies, chanting, nature worship, and house churches. I wanted to ponder both sides.

The school of religion provided a place to ponder, read, and talk with others also captivated by matters called spiritual. I moved like a mariner in easy waters from small apartment to library to classes. I found some gay activists committed to social justice and Asian students talking of "buffalo theology." I found a professor interested in religious humor and one who taught Christian ethics. I poured over the materials and imagined myself on the way to inner peace.

Instead of gentle sailing I had a barnacle stuck to my hull, my rebellious daughter. No, that's not the image. My daughter was more like a runner chasing me as I tried to walk with measured steps through the gothic corridors of my beautiful seminary. She wouldn't attend school and turned to smoking God knows what and hanging out at LaVal's Pizza with runaways and truants. We battled over absences from home, hatred of school, and episodes of stealing. She was arrested, found driving a stolen pickup, and had drug paraphernalia in her bedroom. I was in constant contact with the police and had to fight the urge to send her to her father, who didn't want her.

I was never left to myself, it seemed. I never could get far from harsh words and the dark streets where I'd search for Margaret. I came to despise the other students, the ones without children, the ones who were free of the suffering I endured. I made every class assignment—whether it was for religion and politics or a counseling seminar—about my wild daughter and how difficult it was to raise her. If I'd had a hair shirt, I'd have worn it.

The daily coping, the trying to keep my daughter safe, burned away my defenses until I went from a capable, tidy person to a vulnerable, tearful, frantic person. I had to get help. I turned to a therapist for a while. I studied and prayed with a woman who'd written a book I liked, *Prayer and Our Inner Wounds*. I felt a naked yearning for peace, for reassurance, and for meaning in the upheaval at home.

Three years passed, and my path took me into ministry—my own version of the priesthood, you could say. I finished my studies alive and sane, Margaret at my side. She grew into a competent young woman—a skeptical realist, a defensive driver, and a fine hairdresser—and her transformation happened by the grace of God. She went off to find her way, and I was assigned a small church in northern Arizona. By the time I got there, I'd learned how to preach about the struggle to be good. I knew what failure and guilt can do to the spirit, and I'd found how to forgive myself and others. Nothing that happened in that beautiful Arizona ranch country surprised me. I'd raised a teenager.

The mystics tell us that struggle—even failure—brings spiritual insight. It's pleasant to think my struggles have brought insight, but I desired a crown, not the sour taste of inadequacy. I do have the occasional realization, though, and here's my favorite: spirituality does not come from books offering definitions of God. Great perceptions do not come from yoga class and meditation. Spirituality—compassion, awareness and tolerance—comes with chasing and worrying until defenses drop away like old boots and you stand in bare feet.

ELAINE GREENSMITH JORDAN is a retired Congregational minister and former high-school teacher. Now living in Arizona, her soul still resides in California, especially on the coast. Her essays have been published in small journals, and she has an unpublished memoir of her ministry on her desk. She received the Nonfiction Prize, 2005, from the Preservation Foundation.

Entrances and Exits

Life is no brief candle to me, it is a sort of splendid torch which I've got hold of for the moment and I want to make it burn as brightly as possible before handing it on to future generations
—GEORGE BERNARD SHAW

All my life's a circle, sunrise and sundown,
Moon rolls through the night time, 'til the daybreak comes around
All my life's a circle, though I can't tell you why
Seasons spinning 'round again, the years keep rolling by
—HARRY CHAPIN

LIFE IS A SERIES OF PASSAGES, and it is indeed a circle through which we will all pass more than once. Life is meant to be a chance to obtain an education, like going to school, and hopefully, not being left back but advancing through the grades. When I give a report in Heaven, which I often do since I am an outside consultant to the board of directors, I conclude my report with the prescribed words, "The Beginning." At first I foolishly questioned this, asking why not "The End"? God explained that when you graduate from school, it is called a "commencement," not a "termination," and the Bible ends in a "Revelation," not a "Conclusion." So life is a series of beginnings or passages. Whether we learn something, experience a change, or lose something, we are to begin a new life. That is why God didn't create a perfect world—so we can live and learn.

God further reminded me that we are all here to live, learn, and move up through the grades as we acquire wisdom till our bodies cease to exist. Then we can pass on through our consciousness, which never ceases to exist, what we have learned and experienced, hopefully enhancing life rather than detracting from it. But remember, becoming angry at third graders accomplishes nothing. We must help to educate everyone and lift the level of consciousness. So let your curses become blessings, and keep beginning as you pass through life.

My life has been filled with many interesting passages, the first being my passage through the birth canal into the material world. Due to an illness and my mother's poor state of health, she was told not to become pregnant since it would be a threat to her life. Her mother (my grandmother) decided otherwise, however. She embarked on a mission to help my mother regain her strength and had her lie down on the couch while my grandmother fed her constantly. After my mother gained thirty pounds, I was conceived. The next problem was a multitude of complications of the pregnancy and prolonged labor with no child appearing. According to my mother, after she was told she might not survive a cesarean section, "They reached in and pulled you out."

So my first passage was a very traumatic one, and I was born an ugly duckling. "Your father and I wrapped you in kerchiefs and put you in a carriage, which we covered and hid behind the house so nobody would see you and be upset." When I asked my mom why I didn't turn out to be an addict or alcoholic, which infants treated this way may become, she said, "My mother took you, poured oil all over your body and pushed everything back where it belonged." An infant massaged in this way gains weight 50 percent faster than an infant fed the same amount but not touched. In orphanages in the 1800s, infants were not touched to avoid spreading infections, and 90 percent died because they were not touched. So to pass through life successfully, we need to experience love.

I realize that if we all had loving grandmothers, there wouldn't be any ugly ducklings who have to struggle to discover their beauty, something which most of us never accomplish. So when in doubt, act like a loving grandparent to ease the passages of others. Let your eyes be the mirrors which reflect love and beauty back to those who look into them. Experience reveals that when someone you love is present during labor or any painful experience, the pain experienced is dramatically reduced.

AT AGE FOUR, while sitting on my bed at home due to an ear infection, I almost choked to death on some toy parts I had put into my mouth and then aspirated. I had an NDE, a near death experience, and left my body. I was free of the physical struggle to breathe. It was a fantastic experience for a four-year-old, which left me with no fear of death. I can recall wanting to be dead rather than going back because of the guilt I felt over my parents finding my dead body. Then the boy on the bed vomited, and all the toys came flying out. He began to breathe again, and I was back in his body mad as hell that I did not get my choice. I can remember yelling, "Who did that?" and thinking there must be somebody else in charge of the schedule of passages. The truth is that even the blind see when they have an NDE. I know this from my patients and the research of others. So when you pass from this body, you will become dreamless, unalive, and perfect again.

THE NEXT PASSAGE, which as a surgeon I cannot overlook, is simply passing urine, gas, and feces. If you are born with an intestinal atresia, imperforate anus, or other anomaly, you will learn very quickly what a blessing it is to not have an obstruction to these vital organs and functions. When the anatomical passages are open and functioning, one can then focus on the mental and spiritual ones.

When you do, you realize that all of life is a labor pain. The experiences we encounter, or which are prescribed for us, when confronted with life-threatening illnesses are like the labor pains of self-birth. I tell all my patients and the people I counsel to not do something because someone else prescribes it, but rather do it because it is what is right for you. Seeing chemotherapy as poison or surgery as a mutilation leads to your having more problems than the person who sees them as life-saving gifts from God.

So remember, life is difficult but not unfair. How do I know that? Because everyone is complaining, so it must be fair. If you want to help your children, then prepare them for the difficult passages which we all must confront. If you don't know what to do, here's my mother's advice: Whenever someone you know runs into trouble say, "It was meant to be. God is redirecting you. Something good will come of this." It took me a while to buy the package as a teenager, but I realized many curses have in fact turned into blessings and have redirected my life. My mother's words greased the tight spots in my passage.

DR. SIEGEL retired from general and pediatric surgery in 1989 to speak to patients and their caregivers. In 1978, he originated "Exceptional Cancer Patients," a specific form of individual and group therapy. In 1986, his first book, *Love, Medicine & Miracles* was published, followed by *Peace, Love & Healing* (1989), *How to Live between Office Visits* (1993), *Prescriptions for Living* (1998), *Help Me to Heal* (2003), *365 Prescriptions for the Soul* (2003), and *Smudge Bunny* (2004), a children's book. His most recent titles are *101 Exercises for the Soul* (2005) and *Love, Magic, and Mud Pies* (2006), a book on parenting. In his writing and work, Bernie wants to humanize medical education and medical care and to empower patients to live fully and to die in peace. He continues to break new ground in the field of healing.

PART III

Sea Changes

I am happier this morning thinking

that a reason for my many disappointments

is not so much a lack of productivity

as my need for a much longer life . . .

—CHARLES WELD, A LIFE OF BIBLICAL PROPORTION (p. 21)
See also *Secrets of Heaven* 3696.2, Swedenborg (p. 161).

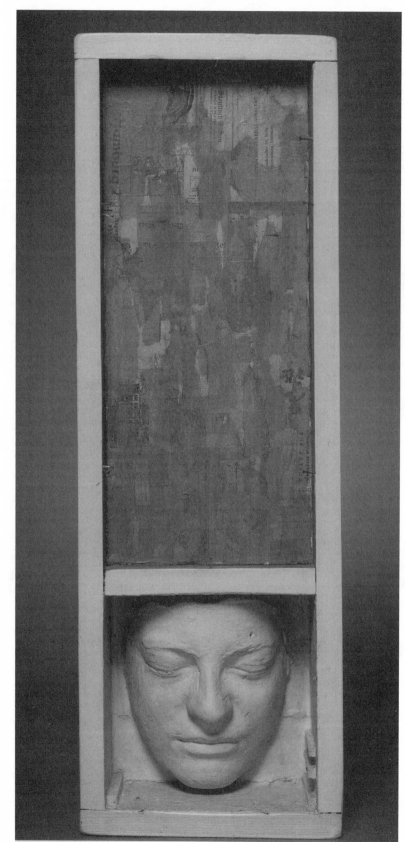

Jasper Johns.
Untitled.
Painted wood,
painted plaster cast,
photomechanical
reproductions on
canvas, glass, and nails,
26¼ x 8⅞ x 4⅜ in.,
1954. Hirshhorn Museum
and Sculpture Garden,
Smithsonian Institution.
Regents Collections
Acquisition Program,
with matching funds
from the
Thomas M. Evans,
Jerome L. Greene,
Joseph H. Hirshhorn, and
Sydney and Frances Lewis
Purchase Fund, 1987.
Photographer
Lee Stalsworth.

Red Earth, Golden Sky

NARROW SLIVERS OF LIGHT bounced off the wing of the plane and seeped through the cracks of the shade, gently awakening me. Rubbing my eyes, I turned to look outside. Morning's first golden rays had transformed the indistinct, gray mass beneath me into a rich, burnt red. It looked like a clay pot just after it's been removed from the kiln. I had never seen earth quite like it—it was parched and scorched, but it had life in it yet. I sensed there were many stories it could tell me, if only I could learn to listen.

But listening never was my strong suit; Sandra always told me that. Sandra was my ex-girlfriend. It was our breakup that brought about this trip. I slid the blind up and dazzling sunshine streamed in. The last solid ground I remembered seeing was the perfectly manicured and watered grass of a baseball diamond somewhere in New Jersey. That was an entire ocean away now. I squinted to make out the ground below. There were no baseball fields down there; that was for sure. The guy beside me was just coming to also. He stretched, peered out the window and said something to me in Swedish. I nodded and gazed back out the window.

There's nothing daring or romantic about entering a country by plane unless your name is Lindbergh. Or the Beatles. With a brand new millennium not far behind, twenty-first-century humankind lives in the ever-growing shadow of our past. Except for the very depths of the sea, the entire planet has been picked over and scoured. Most of the sensational arrivals that could be made have been. The comings and goings of modern man are like a shadow passing over a bridge.

For some reason, I kept thinking of Ferdinand Magellan, the Portuguese explorer commissioned to find a new route to the rich trading ports of the Indies. Though he succeeded in circumnavigating the globe, he never made it back to Spain. He was killed in the Philippines leading a band of sixty sailors into battle against two-thousand native warriors. Juan Sebastian del Cano, who had earlier spearheaded a failed mutiny, was the only one of Magellan's captains to survive the journey. He led the half-starved crew of his ship, the *Victoria,* triumphantly into port at Seville. Of the two-hundred-sixty-five seamen who began the voyage, eighteen survived. With Magellan not around to reveal him for the irresolute mutineer he was, Del Cano and his crew received a hero's welcome.

In Madrid, I took a room in a hostel on a narrow alley off the Puerta del Sol. Directly across the street was a rundown coin laundry. Next door was a fruiteria whose produce was mostly overripe. On the front wall of the hostel was a bronze plaque that announced to the handful of people who found their way down the alley that this was the abode where the famous author Miguel de Cervantes Saavedra spent the last years of his life. Someone once told me that Cervantes was the Shakespeare of Spain. The two great writers actually passed away within a month of each other.

Spain was the most powerful country on earth for nearly a century. Her armada of battleships was considered invincible. During that period, Queen Isabella I and King Ferdinand V funded the Italian navigator Christopher Columbus in his several voyages to what he insisted were the Indies. The man after whom cities and countries would be named and for whom statues and monuments without number have been erected was later jailed on a trumped-up charge that amounted to mismanagement.

In El Parque de Buen Retiro, I met a woman with deep brown eyes and full, sensuous lips that reminded me of Sandra. She invited me to the bullfights, but I declined. It didn't sound like such a fair fight.

After a month in Madrid, I decided to head south. During the bus ride to Granada, one of our tires blew. We pulled to the side of an open stretch of highway. It was blazing hot. I sat on the dusty ground against a chain link fence and let the sun beat down on my face. It felt good.

The driver—a flabby, middle-aged man—was unperturbed by the turn of events. He opened a compartment on the side of the bus and pulled out a spare tire, some tools, and a canvas bag. In front of everyone—young, old, women, and children—he stripped down to his gray, blotchy boxer shorts and removed a pair of khaki, oil-stained coveralls from the bag and stepped into them. Then he systematically went to work on the tire.

About five minutes later, a heavy-set, elderly woman in a brown smock and black shawl came over and asked me in Spanish to help the driver. I pretended I didn't understand.

Isabella and Ferdinand were interred in Granada. It was a political decision. She was from Castile, and he from Aragon. Their marriage merged the two kingdoms and enabled them to drive the Moors from Granada, not to mention the Jews and almost everyone else who didn't share their theo-sociological beliefs. When they died, their home states wanted each of them buried in native soil. They had wed to unite the country; their deaths nearly tore it apart.

In the cathedral at Granada, I caught a street urchin trying to pick my pocket. He was tall and skinny with a long, hooked nose. His dark features made me think he was one of the gypsies that lived in the caves across from the Alhambra. Feeling a slight tug at my hip pocket, I slapped his hand away and spun around to face him.

Seeing that the jig was up, he feigned imbecility, shouting: "Soy loco, soy loco!"

I thought about bashing his skull in against Isabella's sarcophagus. Instead, I pulled a one-thousand peseta note from my wallet and handed it to him. He accepted it in perplexed silence. Behind him was an el Greco version of La Pieta. In it, the Virgin Mary cradled Jesus's lifeless body as she wept.

At my pension in Granada, I met an Australian who was backpacking her way across Europe. She wore a deep sorrow just beneath her smile, the way Sandra had toward the end. I'd crossed an ocean to get away from her, but everywhere I looked, she was there. The Australian, who couldn't have been more than twenty, had spent the winter cleaning rooms at a ski resort in Switzerland. There she'd fallen deeply in love with a boy from Prague who also worked at the hotel as a bellhop. She told me she had to return to Australia in a few weeks, and she was worried she might never see her young man again. I had no response. I told her that I'd heard that the southern half of Spain would be completely desert within fifty years.

When I returned to Madrid, I fell ill. I curled up in a fetal position on my narrow, single bed. My head throbbed and waves of nausea rolled over me. After three days without eating, I gathered my strength and headed downstairs. I asked the senora—a stout, graying woman who was by turns impatient and irritable, and then sweet and motherly—where I could find a doctor. She knew I had a lot of belongings in my room upstairs, so she must have been afraid I might die before settling my bill because she asked me to pay the balance before leaving. Then she directed me to the nearest hospital.

At the hospital, a chubby, effete man who worked the reception desk explained that they couldn't treat me until I had handed over thirty-five thousand pesetas in cash. I didn't have that kind of money. I wondered if I were to drop dead right then and there, would they have left my body in the lobby to rot or would they at least drag me around back and throw me into a dumpster?

I staggered outside and caught a cab back to my hostel.

The fourth day, I was lying naked on top of rumpled, sweat-soaked sheets. Half delirious from fever and lack of food, I was convinced I could see Cervantes' long, lean body seated at the small writing table against the opposite wall. His narrow back, the back that had been whipped as a galley slave in his youth, was hunched forward, and his withered left arm had been placed delicately atop the table. He was writing something. A new wave of nausea gripped me, and my head began to throb as I propped myself up on my elbows for a better look. Turning to me, a wan smile spread across his gaunt, deeply lined face. Though the smile was sad, infinitely sad, it lacked all bitterness or contempt. I blinked to make sure I wasn't hallucinating, and he was gone.

The fifth day, I still hadn't eaten, and the fever continued to rage. The prospect of dying in a tiny room, thousands of miles from home became alarmingly real. By that time, it wasn't even the idea of dying that bothered me. What I found I couldn't understand was why it had to take so long.

The next day, the fever broke.

I decided right then to write it all down—every detail. That way I wouldn't forget anything, like the way I'd already begun to forget Sandra. The smell of her perfume, the taste of her lips, the feel of her skin; it had all slipped away from me, bit by bit, in less than one year. This time I wanted to save it, all of it, the bad and the good. When I put the pen to paper, all that would come out was: "Red earth, golden sky . . ."

———

STEPHEN GRAF has been published by numerous literary and consumer magazines, such as *The Mountain Laurel*, *AIM Magazine*, *The Black Mountain Review* (in Ireland), *Cicada*, *The Southern Review*, and *Fiction* magazine. Originally from Pittsburgh, he has lived and worked in Madrid and is currently pursuing a doctorate in twentieth-century Irish literature at the University of Newcastle-upon-Tyne in England.

The Last Atheist

My history professor at Rutgers proclaims
at an all-night teach-in,
"I welcome a Vietcong victory in Vietnam."
Bumper stickers react: Rid Rutgers of Reds.
Years later, having found Jesus,
he speaks more of Christ than the Cong.
The latest on Jane Fonda
says she is Born Again.
If Jesus were born again,
Mary and Joseph would find
appropriate day care.
A soccer mom, Mary drives
her kid from field to fastfood.
Christ contemplates Columbine,
suffers with the communists
and the children of Palestine.

RONALD F. SMITS is a professor of English at Indiana University of Pennsylvania and lives in Ford City, Pennsylvania. His poems have appeared or are forthcoming in *North American Review, Poetry East, Poet Lore, The South Carolina Review, The Southern Review, Tar River Poetry, The Texas Observer,* and many other journals and anthologies.

Not Quite

———————————————————————————

TO SAVE THE BABY, Leslie had left work three weeks ago. Since then, she mostly lay with feet elevated on pillows hoping to stop the bleeding. Tonight that position was so uncomfortable, she moved her head to the bottom of the bed and propped her feet against the wall. Beside her face were Don's hairy knees. For an hour he was motionless, like someone in suspended animation. She felt that way herself. Not quite pregnant, not quite married, but somewhere just short of each.

Earlier, Don had ushered Leslie to bed and rubbed her lower back to ease the pain. She wished he would stroke her gently, but he went after the ache as if sanding old paint from a table. He patted her shoulder and said, "Don't keep anything from me," then efficiently dropped off to sleep. And how will I tell you? she thought.

When her knees hurt, she eased her feet down. The little life inside her struggled to hang on. It didn't know how to grow into her. Was she ready herself? Her own mother had died when Leslie was three, and she felt as though she lacked some instinct other women had, as if she had never been attached herself. She curled around one of the pillows. Hold on like this, she told the baby. We'll hold on together and won't let go.

Twenty minutes later she woke shivering. She cramped and felt a drip on the back of her thigh. She started up, felt woozy, and sat down. It was more than spotting now. She shuffled to the bathroom. "Don!" she called. "Don!" There was a fuddled crash. "We have to go to the hospital." The doctor had warned her of the danger of hemorrhaging. But she would not tell Don that. He would go berserk.

"Damn!" After more crashing, Don shouted into the telephone, "Bleeding! Yes, dammit! Bleeding!" He clunked her packed bag through the house, heading for the garage.

Why didn't he rush to her, wrap an arm around her waist, tell her everything would be okay? As Leslie emerged on the porch, Don squealed the Dodge to a stop, leapt out, flung open the back door. "More room here. They said to lie flat." Leslie slid in gingerly while he jumped into the driver's seat and thunked into reverse. He backed into the street and braked so sharply, she nearly rolled onto the floor.

Flashers pulsing, Don tore through the city streets. He honked and blinked high beams as he ran stop signs and red lights. "Not so fast, Don. You're scaring me."

"Every minute counts," he said. It was as if they were driving to separate destinations.

At the hospital they wheeled her past hallway doors so fast she felt dizzy. "I hate to put you in the maternity ward," an older nurse said, "but it has the facilities you need." Leslie barely heard. When she closed her eyes, images of neon signs and tops of telephone poles blurred past. The sheets were cold, and her body wouldn't warm them. She gripped the mattress with both hands to hang on. Hanging on was all she did. She had felt that way for years.

The hospital team weighed her pads every hour to determine blood loss, and her doctor said that if it exceeded a certain rate, they would have to abort. Don sat expectantly the first hours, high-strung, lit-up from his race across the city. His anxiety was not personal for her. He could equally rush into a burning building to save a trapped dog. His excitement arose and vanished from his own inner demons. As hours of routine passed, though, he grew quieter, bored. He counted the ceiling tiles, then calculated the number of holes in the ceiling tiles. Pretty soon he'd multiply that by the number of rooms in the hospital and that by the number of hospitals in the world so he'd know all the holes that were. As he counted, the older nurse, whose name was Linda, returned to let Leslie know her shift had ended. "I'll be in tomorrow," she said. "Wait for me." Leslie nodded.

IN THE MORNING new doctors and nurses invaded the room. What did it matter if she bled three ounces or three quarts? Did they understand that a little life was trying to hold onto her? Leslie felt nasty, snapped at them like a harassed animal. When Don paced, she ordered him to leave the room.

The bleeding slowed, and Leslie finally warmed up. When the doctors said things were "stable," Don told her, "We'll have that baby yet." He patted her hand to assure her.

"Don't be an idiot. Do you really think this is going to turn out well?"

"I bought a newspaper downstairs. Want me to read you the news? Do the Jumble together?"

"The Jumble?" What did he think they had been doing? She shook her head and shut her eyes while he read to himself. She imagined each turning page was wind rustling meadow grass. She concentrated on the swishing and fell asleep. When she woke, Don slept in the chair, the paper dripping from his lap. Poor man, Leslie thought. I'm awfully hard on him. Why should he know how to do this? He hasn't even figured out how to have a wife yet. She peeked at her pad. Dry.

That afternoon heavy bleeding and the cold shakes returned. Nurses piled blankets on her and examined her pad every twenty minutes. One whispered to another, "shock." One blessing: Linda had returned. She gently rubbed Leslie's back and said, "Relax, dear. Just relax the shakes away." Her voice was kind and soothing.

An hour later, Leslie's legs trembled uncontrollably, and she cramped hard. Within minutes, they wheeled her to a delivery room, lifted her feet to the stirrups and sedated her. But Leslie wasn't asleep, just unable to move. She wanted them to pour more stuff into her IV—knock her out so she knew nothing. But she couldn't speak.

As the doctor worked, she felt nothing—but almost would have preferred pain. She had been afraid to be pregnant, but she wanted the baby now. What were these people doing between her legs? She felt herself melting. Inky fog rose around her, muffling the doctors and nurses. It was like warm, inky water, and she knew death had come for her. When it covered her and hushed the voices, she heard a tiny, vague sound like whispering grasses. The baby's voice, whispering something just beyond the edge of words. She! It was a she! She didn't sound frightened or angry at dying. She was just whispering to herself as she faded into nothing. She sounded almost happy at being spared life.

Wait! Leslie pleaded. I'll go with you. I don't want to stay here alone. She felt herself rise. The grip of the stirrups and pressure on her back lessened. The inky tide buoyed her toward the tiny voice. Was the baby truly content to go? Was it okay not to live? To not quite live? She wanted to know, to see her baby. The tide had raised Leslie to the ceiling, and she saw the doctors below working on her own body. They were anxious and intense. She'd never seen herself this way before and was surprised at how ordinary, how limp and tired, her flesh seemed. She saw Don in the waiting room too. He glanced at his watch and tapped the rolled newspaper against his leg. His wife was dying, and he had no idea! She laughed. It was all so silly. What did Don and she have to do with each other? Two years married and he didn't sense this extraordinary experience happening to her?

What did she have to do with hospitals, family, or life? She never belonged here. Since her mother died, Leslie had felt orphaned. Now that she was light, she realized how heavy she had been when alive. The real Leslie had cringed inside the heavy flesh people mistook for her. No one told her death would release you to float as you were intended. It was not eerie but more like she had found something she lost long ago, and she went with it, as trusting as a child.

As she relaxed, she softened and dispersed, atomized like smoke. Fear, resentment, and pettiness drained from her pores. Bills, her house, and the squabble with Aunt Jill drained out. She grew lighter. Don was seeping away, then even the loss she felt for her mother. She was spreading into the air, flowing down the hospital corridors and escaping through its windows and doors like gas. Outside was a cold, clear night with stars as clean as crystal. She flowed into it, felt her fingers stretch into long, sinuous clouds and her fingertips extend to touch ten stars. Her baby was there too, ahead of her, whispering singsong baby gurgles as she dissolved into the night. What would be left when all Leslie knew and owned and remembered was gone? She didn't care. As each piece of her life departed, she felt lighter and happier, more herself than ever. This was not death at all, but life at last.

A bump jarred her. The kind a canoe makes lurching over a rock in the current. What hard thing could be up here? Then the tide receded. It lowered her toward the hospital below, and Leslie eddied as through a funnel back into the operating room toward her inert flesh on the table. As the funnel narrowed, it squeezed her together again, returning her weight to her. She tried to hold herself up, but her hands were like fog, could grasp nothing. She slid down toward that woman she had been, down the warm, black, silky funnel until the table was imminent.

LESLIE! HER SHOULDER SHOOK. "Leslie!" It was Linda, the nurse. "You've been gone four hours." Leslie groaned, struggling to keep her eyes from rolling. Dizziness nauseated her.

Don said, "Ready to go bowling?"

"What?" Leslie's mouth was cottony and thick.

"Want to go bowling?" He had pasted on a cheery grin, and Leslie slowly focused on his unshaven chin. He could have been a man in a bus station. She turned her head away.

"I was just kidding. . . ." He slumped like a flat tire.

Linda said to Don, "Listen, I have to do some things here. Why don't you grab a bite to eat. It's nearly midnight." When Don obeyed, the nurse sat on the bed and took Leslie's hand. "Now, close your eyes and come back again—slower."

Leslie shut her eyes. The darkness seemed ordinary now. "The baby's—gone?"

"Yes."

She kept her eyes closed. "Was it a boy or girl?"

"Not a good question, honey."

"I know it was a girl. She talked to me."

"Oh? Just remember that when the body rejects it, there's usually something wrong. This way is best."

"I rejected her?"

"Let's say your body knew the baby wasn't ready to live."

"She didn't care. She wasn't sad at all. She was singing as she floated away. Don would think I was loopy if I told him that. He'd say it was the anesthesia. He doesn't feel anything."

"She spoke to you?"

"It was black and calm. Nothing bothered me. I wanted to follow the baby. We were going to be together. Everything was going to be together. It was like I escaped death when I died. They thought I was dead, didn't they?"

"Yes, they did."

"That's funny because I felt alive and free. But I got heavy and fell back into myself." She smiled. "It sounds so mystical."

"Tell your husband."

"Why?"

"Try." Linda stroked Leslie's forearm.

"He wasn't here for me! He had no idea! He ought to know something!"

"Why should he know what it feels like? You're just learning yourself."

Leslie nodded. That was true. "I didn't have a mother to tell me anything—"

"No woman knows until it happens. And afterward, we forget—or we'd never have another child." Her stroking raised goose bumps on Leslie's arm. It felt good. She wished Linda would never stop.

Leslie asked, "Did the baby die because I didn't want her hard enough?"

"No, dear." Linda slid closer so her uniform nearly touched Leslie's face. "No."

Leslie sniffed faint perfume cutting through the uniform's hospital scents. How nice it would be to lie against her, pulled close and cradled like a baby herself. When Linda guided Leslie's head to her lap, it was as if she knew her mind. Leslie settled into the warmth and whispered, "Some mother-to-be!"

"It's fine, dear. I seldom have the chance to be a real nurse." Leslie gripped a fold of uniform and pressed her face to Linda's hip. "I know you'll be back next year with a baby." Leslie shook her head. Was that possible? Not with Don. Never! She felt Linda's breaths and breathed in sync with her. She kept her eyes shut, suspended in the quiet hospital night. She would not reopen them. This wasn't as good as floating on that silky tide, but it was better than anything else here. She knows, Leslie thought. She knows me. Linda said, "Having a miscarriage doesn't make you less a woman, any more than popping out a baby makes you a real mother."

"I don't feel like anything now, except maybe mush."

"I know. I had two miscarriages before my kids were born."

Leslie snuggled closer. Poor Linda. She did this twice? And tried again? She patted Linda's leg. At the sound of footfalls, she opened her eyes. Don froze in the doorway at the sight of her on Linda's lap, then backpedaled into the hall. He's afraid he'll have to comfort me! Leslie thought. She shut her eyes and sank back. "Did you feel your babies go away like I did?"

"No. I wish I had the chance to say goodbye. Maybe I'm in obstetrics to find my own lost ones." She smoothed the hair on Leslie's forehead. Leslie smiled weakly. Linda rose and bent to a low shelf on her rolling tray. "Tomorrow they'll discharge you along with the new mothers and babies. It's not right, but it's how they do it. Here." She placed a small bouquet of mixed flowers in Leslie's arms. "You must have something to carry out too."

"Thank you." Leslie pictured that moment in the lobby as infants were handed to beaming new mothers and fathers. She would be empty and walk out alone. But she would do it. She would not ever settle for death again.

Linda said, "I'll put them in water overnight." The petals were cool and smooth and greenhouse scented. There were daisies, carnations, and one not-quite-opened pink rose.

M. GARRETT BAUMAN is the author of *Ideas and Details,* a popular college writing textbook. A frequent contributor to Chryalis Reader, his work has also appeared in *Yankee, Sierra, The New York Times,* and many literary journals. The inspiration for this story came from two lines by Walt Whitman: "Has anyone supposed it lucky to be born? / I hasten to inform him or her it is just as lucky to die."

Smuckers
Makes My Jam

Ivan Albright.
The Farmer's Kitchen.
Oil on canvas,
36 x 30⅛ in.,
ca. 1934. Smithsonian
American Art Museum.
Transfer from the U.S.
Department of Labor.

I USED TO BAKE EVERY LOAF OF BREAD WE EVER ATE. It was always whole grain with honey, not sugar. We ate brown rice with ground sesame seeds, bulgur with pinto beans, oatmeal with raisins. I made yogurt and put up jams and jellies. Remember the currants I got from Garda? She had kept her bushes back during the blight when everyone was required to destroy them. Illegal currants!

I used to fix the car myself—just open the hood and see what was wrong in there, spark plugs in my hand, grease under my nails.

Wood was the only heat, warming us from that top-load Ashley. The logs came in 4-foot lengths. He sawed them up, and I split them. Once I got the hang of it, I loved splitting those logs, swinging the maul high above my head and smashing it into the grain of the log. The heat from those logs was so much more satisfying than the heat that now blows out of the floor and warms the air. That heat from the woodstove could skip the air; it heated us directly, right through the clothes, right down to the skin and into the bones.

I'm reminded of those days as I rake the leaves that have fallen from the huge old maples in my yard, brown and yellow leaves mostly, hardly any orange and no red this year. They've gotten duller and maybe I have too.

I never bake bread anymore. I quit the day we split up. Nope, I haven't kneaded a ball of dough since. Arnold's bakes my bread for me now. Columbo makes my yogurt. The woodstove makes good back-up heat when the world outside dips below freezing, but the wood comes to me already cut and split by a machine.

Remember the shed I built from scratch for the chickens? Now the chickens are long gone. I get my eggs from Shaw's Supermarket. And the shed itself has seen better days, the roof leaking and the floor buckling. That shed needs repairs I would once have done myself, but now I'm hiring someone to do it. I still know how. I still could do it myself. I could still bake bread and make preserves. I could grow pot and sew quilts. I could chop wood and carry water. I could if I would, but I won't. I'm not that person anymore. I don't want to do those things. It's enough to know that if survival depended on it, I could do them. I have the knowledge, the experience, the know-how to do them. But I don't miss them.

Now I'm having a good time being who I am today, reading and writing in a furnace-warmed home. I like going to work in an office instead of toiling in a rustic kitchen, turning on a faucet when I want water, taking my car to the mechanic, leaving my hands clean to use the computer, making mosaics, and scratching my cat under her chin.

These memories of a woman I once was are like visiting an old friend, and that was just one of me. I'll bet there's a whole bunch more visiting I could do with people I used to be. I know them all so well, a fine bunch, me.

CHARLENE WAKEFIELD is a writer and visual artist living in Westminster, Vermont. She has been published in Chrysalis Reader, The *Best of Write Action,* and *The Cracker Barrel.* Her artwork, a piece created from broken dishes, appeared on the cover of the Reader *Chances Are . . . .*

The First Peugeot of Spring

We split
  years ago
issues   mostly personal
  some automotive
In the end it was
cold steel
  an '89 grey Peugeot
that came between us

It was hers
  she loved it
beyond reason
  never drove it
in winter   annexed
my CRX instead

Now   as the ides
of March approaches
  I look for the car
to appear again
  dust-covered
in the small parking lot
near her office

ART STEIN, a semi-retired architect, lives with his artist spouse, Margaret, in Northfield, Massachusetts. His free verse has appeared in *Sahara, BOGG* (U.K.), *Faquier, Tundra,* and *Poetry Motel.* His haiku, senryu, and tanka appear frequently in journals devoted to those Japanese forms in English. Art is a founding member of the publishing collective, Slate Roof, committed to providing publishing opportunities for poets in western Massachusetts.

Under New Management

THE PROBLEM HAD BECOME AN INDUSTRIAL NIGHTMARE: we just could not make two products critical to the entire Korean War effort, the F-5 autopilot and VGI vertical guidance indicator. The U.S. Air Force had several hundred new Sabre-Jets parked outside the aircraft plant in California and more being built every day, stuck in place and useless because of our plant's inability to produce and satisfy way overdue delivery promises.

These fighter aircraft were so fast that they could not be piloted without our F-5 autopilot and the VGI vertical gyro instrument. Our company, The Prince Corporation (all names disguised), was being blamed for grounding planes urgently needed for fighting the Korean War. There was no escaping the facts of our failure and its serious consequences. U.S. Air Force generals and top U.S. Defense Department officials flocked over our plant to try to determine what was wrong and get it fixed.

But we knew what was wrong and did not need their help. We just couldn't fix it. At least right away, because it was not just a simple fix. It was hundreds of problems.

Parts were being rejected because the tooling for making them was designed badly, sub-assemblies would not fit together, dimensions were in error, vendors were not able to deliver because the blueprints and specifications kept being changed, engineering change-orders were pouring into process designers by the dozens every day, and when an occasional product was finally assembled, it would not perform as designed and was rejected. It was a total, discouraging, disastrous mess.

We had a new product, a new plant, new machine tools, new employees, new processes, new production planning and control systems, and dozens of new managers. All this newness was because of an explosion of demand for the advanced, high-tech aeronautical products that our division of the Prince Corporation had proven ourselves to be highly capable of producing in the past.

Our very success led the U.S. Air Force, our key customer, to come to us and literally command us to double the size and capacity of our facility to produce the F-5 and the VGI, and under enormous time pressure. The products were so important that the U.S. Air Force wanted to set us up as a second source for these products, originally designed and sold to the U.S. Air Force by our number one competitor, the McAlpin Corp.

We did not want to accept this task, partly because it would be aiding our competitor to penetrate a market we had hitherto dominated, and partly because the products were still being designed and the schedules were clearly going to be virtually impossible to meet.

But the government applied heavy pressure, offered to provide us with all necessary machine tools, build a new building attached to our present building, and added a strong measure of patriotism. Our top management gave in, of course, and agreed to take on the project.

It was an exciting time, for we were to double the size of the plant, the number of machines and machinists, assembly workers, all support groups, such as quality control, production control, process engineering, and sales volumes. Very shortly after agreeing to accept this order, construction contracts were signed, concrete was poured within weeks, and a new management cadre was interviewed, and hirings began at a fast clip.

The F-5/VGI project was so big and our "regular" products were selling so well and expanding volumes continually that it was decided to set up the McAlpin Program, as it came to be called, as a separate organization in parallel with the "regular" organization. It was hoped that the McAlpin team would bring new ideas and systems which would benefit the whole Aero Division. The management team which was hired in from all over the country came with outstanding credentials and was selected with great care and intensive interviewing. As a result, while they were new to us "regulars," they were clearly able and very impressive managers, and with excellent, relevant experience.

They went at their work with high spirits, cooperated with each other, and invested energy and ideas at a high rate. Amongst themselves they were often critical of the more conventional and less "advanced" system and management approaches used in the well established regular organization. Not surprisingly the two organizations

became (quietly at first and more openly later) competitive and ultimately defensive of their production systems and results.

But the results began to contrast as the McAlpin team ran into
the massive problems described earlier, while the regular team set
new records. Despite the new team's strong capabilities, efforts, and
initially high morale, they could not produce F-5s and VGIs and a
sense of emergency, crisis, and frustration soon set in. Six months of
desperate efforts solved dozens of problems with the parts designs
and processes. There weren't dozens of problems: there were hundreds and hundreds of problems. Hardly anything worked the first
time, and the team worked harder and harder as nights and weekends
became a normal pattern.

Top management, of course, pounced in, applying pressure and
ideas. Plant Manager Henry Ellis, who himself had been hired from
GE only several years before the McAlpin Project, began to criticize
the new team (which had been reporting to him from the start).
Managers in the regular organization who had been competing with
the new group took pleasure in their failures. They pointed out to
Ellis the mistakes the new managers were making, and shortly he
fired several of the men who had been hired for the project.

A team was dispatched to visit the McAlpin plant to see how they
were doing with the same new products. They found to their delight
but also their disappointment that McAlpin could be of no help
whatsoever. They were having the same massive, totally disastrous
problems that we were having.

My job was as assistant to the plant manager. In this position I
worked with both the old group and the new group. I came to respect
many of the new managers and heard of their frustrations and com-
plaints about the regular team's managers, systems, and attitudes.
They felt that they had never been accepted as equals by the regular
team's managers, and when cooperation in the use of facilities and
workers was needed, it was often denied.

The alienation between the two groups grew worse as the new
group slipped further and further behind in the schedule, and the nation's war-effort pressures intensified on the Prince Company.

After another few months of failure, Henry Ellis, with the con-
currence of Lewis Trane, the operations manager over production
and engineering to whom he reported, decided on a total reorgani-
zation of Aero Production. Each and every management function in
the McAlpin organization would report to the head of that function
in the regular organization. In effect, this abolished the separate
McAlpin operation by placing it all under the old, regular team. The
regulars, the old-timers had won. The competition was over.

The regulars were pleased and felt that their successes on the Prince products had been recognized and that the upstart outsiders had been shown to be less able than their outstanding resumes had promised.

In the McAlpin team the organizational change was terribly disappointing. Each man now had to report into an old, long established group; they lost their sense of independence and freedom to make decisions and innovate. Of about eight at the top of their group, five left Prince within several months. (Their top man stayed on, however, and accepted his new role with apparent grace and a cooperative spirit.)

The smug rejoicing of the regular team was short-lived. They, of course, now had to shoulder the responsibility for the F-5/VGI for the first time and at once became the culprits and management failures for the still disastrous project.

Ellis himself was in the worst position of all. Before, he could blame the inexperienced new McAlpin team and ask top management to give them more time to get things back on track. But now

Wickham Skinner.
*Under New
Management.*
Pen-and-ink,
2006.

that he had placed the project under his seasoned, regular, successful managers, he could not use that excuse for further failures.

Under this intensive spotlight, all the way up to the Pentagon and the White House, Ellis turned up the heat on himself and his people. He showed no panic or temper but got involved more personally in all parts and assembly problems. He demanded action, explanations, fixes, and results.

Among his subordinates the heat was on. They dug into every detail, isolating problems and causes and fixing more dozens of individual problems. The plant manager held meetings in his large office three times weekly for about three hours at a time with twenty to thirty managers in attendance, each prepared to explain what was being done on each problem. Generally the problems were identified by part numbers, and each meeting covered about a hundred parts.

Under all this pressure and the firings of some key people, some of the nine regular managers began to show their tempers, blame each other for the falldowns occurring, and try to defend themselves and their organizations in meetings and with Ellis.

Antagonisms were especially common between production control and parts manufacturing, and between quality control and assembly. Relationships were tense, and with some backbiting and blaming and complaining. With the long hours and sixty-hour work weeks and yet continued poor results, tempers grew short, and the spirit in the previously successful organization soured day by day.

Little by little a few of each set of products were completed, accepted, and shipped. But the numbers were tiny: where three hundred or more sets were needed, we were only producing about three a week and the rate of increase was not encouraging.

One day maintenance workers wheeled in a cart with a desk and installed it in the plant manager's office side by side with Ellis' desk. It was for the operations manager, his boss Lewis Trane, who immediately moved from his office an eighth of a mile away, to sit beside the plant manager. My office was next door, but I did not dare to walk into the plant manager's office, as I had always done. For two days Trane was present all day in everything that Ellis did.

On the third day I was way out in the plant checking on something for about an hour. When I returned to report to Henry Ellis, I stopped at his door before entering and looked through the window into his office. I saw to my amazement that the office was filled with the top twenty or so of our production management team. Ellis was not there. Mr. Trane was talking to the group assembled. He looked very serious.

It was obvious that Henry Ellis was gone, probably fired, and the managers were being given the news.

I hesitated about going in. My rank was appropriate to those inside, but I had apparently not been invited. Was I as Ellis' assistant getting fired too? Scary, but, of course, I could not go in, so I waited in my office for about fifteen minutes until the meeting was dismissed.

Then I learned that Ellis had been fired (I had been invited to the meeting, but the secretary had not been able to find me). I never saw Ellis again.

Mr. Trane had announced that the director of labor relations for the corporation, John Rind, would take Ellis' place as plant manager. Rind was about forty-eight, had been a successful plant manager at one of Prince's commercial product plants and had been promoted to run labor relations only about eighteen months before. It was considered that he was doing an excellent job. He had a reputation for being tough, firm, open, likeable, and smart in a practical way.

He also had a reputation for having a good sense of humor, but when he came to work the very next day after Trane's announcement, he looked very serious and was not smiling. He was clearly under the enormous pressure of taking charge of a major, broadly discussed bottleneck in the production of vital equipment for the Korean War. He had to succeed somehow where all his predecessors had failed. Most of us knew him, so introductions at his first meeting were very brief. He said little other than that he would sit down with each of us over the next few days and try to learn what was going on.

For ten days he never smiled. He spent his time interviewing the top eight managers in the plant plus engineering managers and men who had been dealing with McAlpin. In my interview he asked question after question but never indicated what he was learning or concluding. He thanked me for my conclusions and analysis. He spent at least two hours with each of us. On the tenth day he sent word to each of us to meet with him at 0800 the next morning.

We assembled around a table in his office. He was as serious and unsmiling as ever. It was very quiet. He then said that he had met at length with each of us. He told us that no one was to be transferred or fired. Instead, he said, he had never met a more competent and proficient group of production people, and each of us in our professional function was outstanding. He knew the problems we had were massive and difficult. He felt we could resolve them one by one and get those planes flying. But, he said, "you have not been working well together. You have not been a real team. There has been fear, defensiveness, mistrust, and hesitation at honest communication. If that goes on we will all fail. You will, we will, work as a team. No one will succeed unless we all succeed together. We will meet every morning around this table for thirty minutes or less to discuss and resolve together the key problems that are hurting us. Everyone will have a chance to speak up. We will work together. We will make decisions together. When we can't agree I will decide. But whatever we decide, we will then all be loyal and totally support that decision when we leave this room. *Is that clear?*"

It was dead quiet. He looked each of us in the eye one by one, all around the table. And we all said "yes." Then he smiled for the first time, and we left the room.

Well, we did begin to work as a team, to cooperate, trust, talk, listen. Part of it was, I'm sure, the fact that no one was going to be fired. We had nowhere to go but up, each of us. Part of it was the consciousness we all felt that cooperation and teamwork was fruitful and that's what our boss demanded. We liked him, respected him, and wanted to please him.

But it was still an exercise in solving hundreds and hundreds of manufacturing, engineering, and high-tech problems. The work pace and pressure continued at a nearly impossible level.

Readers:
Please pause for a moment before reading further. Ask yourself what do you think will happen? Will it just be the same? Or now a happier team though still struggling? Or will they solve those problems and get the planes flying?

Outcome:
After one month the products began to trickle out steadily. After two months we were producing a steady stream and had sixty planes flying. After three months the F-5s and the VGIs were pouring out of the plant, and the crisis was over. In one year we went from an annual sales rate of $10 million to $80 million.

Readers:
Now please pause again and consider some questions: How much of this ultimate success was due to John Rind? Was placing the operation "under new management" really necessary? Was Henry Ellis made the "scapegoat"? Did he have to be fired? Would this group of eight capable managers not have solved these problems soon anyway? What do you think?

WICKHAM SKINNER is the James E. Robison Professor of Business Administration Emeritus at Harvard University, where he was a member of the faculty for twenty-eight years. Prior to his academic career, he was employed in industry and participated in the events described in this article.

SHAWN PITTARD

We All Get That Feeling Sometimes

The fox's head came off cleanly with one sharp blow of the spade.
I winced, but to my Uncle Bud this was simply another chore.
We'll send the head to the University, he said,
shoveling it into the bed of our pickup, kicking
the carcass into the ditch. *They'll know if it's rabid.*

From the safety of the cab, I watched that fox's head.

It rolled to a stop among empty Schmidt's cans, baling wire,
and the gearbox we'd picked up at the mercantile.
There it settled, its red and orange fur
and those long black lips beautiful
against the turquoise and rust of the '36 International.

I studied the bloodshot eyes from behind the glass.

I'd never seen an animal act that way.
In fact, I'd never seen a fox
before I spent that summer on the farm.
But even I could see there was something wrong with him—
standing in the middle of the section road, hair matted
and pointing every which way, tongue hanging
from his panting mouth. On rubbery legs, he watched
us bring the truck to a stop, not bothering to run.

Shooting him seemed like the right thing to do.

But then this morning, moving deeper
into my own middle age, I saw that fox's look
staring back at me from my shaving mirror. A look
I'd seen in the face of a boxer, his corner man
pushing him to his feet to answer the bell.

I wondered if that fox shared our common thought—

I just need a minute   to catch my breath
then I'll get back to it   just another minute
that's all I need

SHAWN PITTARD is the author of *These Rivers*, a chapbook of poems from Rattlesnake Press (2004). His poems and stories have appeared in *Cimarron Review*, *Confrontation*, *Slipstream*, and *Spillway*. He contributes book reviews and essays on poetry and the arts to *The Great American Pinup*—an online blog—from his home in Sacramento.

STEVE WHITAKER

What's the Level?

THERE ARE DEADLY RAPIDS four miles from the White House. I first ran them at the age of twelve to get my parents' attention. They were busy with Watergate, when many of their friends were going to jail. Between televised hearings, I saw a local hippie kayaking the Grand Canyon on *American Sportsman,* with Curt Gowdy following in a raft. A week and fifteen bucks later, I was in the back of that hippie's VW bus headed up Canal Road. His name was Tom McEwan. I may have been his first paying customer. I was wearing a hockey jersey, windbreaker, corduroy flairs, Converse All-Stars, and was expected to maneuver a borrowed thirteen-foot monster. One look at the flooded river made my hair lift. To this day, the smell of effluent reminds me of Richard Nixon.

Paddling the Potomac is, to borrow a term from James Joyce—scrotumtightening. I fear being trapped underwater more than death itself and have been sick with terror all the thirty years since my first descent. I can hold my breath for two minutes, but flip me over and I panic in thirty seconds.

Having seen the death toll of politics, I have always been afraid of it, too. At a very young age, I saw the trappings of official Washington—the Navy driver waiting in the limo before our house, prime seats at the Inauguration, field trips into the Oval Office, Camp David. Around the dinner table, I also heard of the dangers—subpoenas, dirty tricks, CREEP, Lompoc Prison.

It terrified me.

Opposite:
Sarah Anderson.
Potomac River
at high water
near Washington, D.C.
Photograph, 2004.

TOM MCEWAN WAS ALREADY A LOCAL LEGEND for paddling during Hurricane Agnes in 1972, when the Potomac pumped twice as much water as the Mississippi in a channel half the size. The river's surface flowed 3 feet above the C&O Canal towpath, which is normally a half mile inland. The frustrated water drowned Great Falls and squeezed through Mather Gorge like an egg passing through a snake. One of Tom's fellow kayakers missed her roll and swam. The current was moving at more than 30 miles per hour. They saved her, pulled her to shore just above a 20-foot standing wave at the Brookmont Dam. It was the highest river speed ever recorded anywhere. Ever.

Tom was the first to run Great Falls. That's what I wanted to do. Tom said I wasn't ready. Said a Clorox bottle could run the Falls. It had to be done with experience, done safely, and done with style. I never ran it. Even during a drought, when I could have walked across the river to Virginia, I never ran the Falls.

Tom was grooming a generation of the best paddlers in history, and I was not going to be among them. Even the distant sound of the Potomac made me nervous. I was not worried about dying—only that I might not get my parents' attention. Like many Washingtonians in positions of power, they were focused on more important, national issues.

Just after Watergate, my father had a massive coronary. Then bypass surgery. He spent a long time recovering. To decelerate his life, he moved our family to a fishing village in Nova Scotia. I transferred from Georgetown Prep, surrounded by a golf course, to Yarmouth Consolidated Memorial High School, surrounded by a snowbanked parking lot. It was the first time I had ever been in a classroom without a tie and with girls.

Fortunately, Nova Scotia has as many lakes and rivers as it does land. At a time when there may have been fewer than a thousand kayaks in North America, mine may have been the only one in Nova Scotia. For the next ten years I destroyed my thirteen-foot monster running boulder-clogged Nova Scotia streams, accompanied by friends in aluminum canoes.

My fear of rivers receded.

THE YEARS PASSED. After a string of career U-turns—commodities trader, interpreter, academic—at thirty-two-years old I returned to Washington to confront my fear of politics. My father could not have been happier than to have one of his sons back home and trying his line of work. He arranged interviews with old political hands on both sides of the aisle. The interviews came to nothing. I think my father and his friends were dismayed by the new generation running Washington.

I did finally land a job—the old fashioned way. I walked miles and miles, meeting staffers in the Longworth, Cannon, and Rayburn Buildings. My father's one piece of advice was, "Be careful. These are immature politicians."

Before long, there I was—back on the Potomac, charmingly retro in a long boat in the middle of a short-boat revolution. I was still wearing hockey jerseys. I found Tom McEwan and other top paddlers like Davey and Kathy Hearn, who had stayed on the river and become Olympians and world champions. In the Brookmont neighborhood where they lived, there were more gold medals than in East Berlin.

Soon, I was paddling more than two hundred days each year, half of them with my paddling buddy, Stephen. We cheated death many times over the next decade and kept each other from thinking too much about why we would even want to try.

I traded to shorter and shorter boats, reducing overall length by 5 feet. The short boats gave me control, but the primal fears returned. My father said that my stubby kayak seemed to defy Archimedes Principle, which I took to mean, *You've always lacked common sense.* And my mother left phone messages when it rained floodwater hard, saying, "For God's sake you have children now."

The web page for the river level at Little Falls became my favorite. Some days I would hit it every hour. Yet, I sat out the flood of '96. I showed up. I started to put in. I looked at the serpentine beast of the main channel, and I felt my ass pucker. So, I picked up my kayak and walked back to the car.

Meanwhile downstream at Brookmont, Davey Hearn surfed calmly onto the 20-foot standing wave that Tom McEwan's paddling partner barely missed during Hurricane Agnes. The Miracle Wave had a 100-square-yard bowl, and Davey had waited twenty years for it. He pulled a camera from his life jacket and started taking self-portraits. A Park Service helicopter hovered overhead, the prop wash nearly blowing him over. He was later arrested for refusing to let them rescue him. During the Nixon years, my father oversaw the Park Service when gravity sports like rock climbing and kayaking first became popular. He thought people like Davey Hearn didn't deserve to be saved.

Every year, Hurricane Season coincided with Silly Season—the rush of legislative activity before Congress adjourned. Working first for the U.S. House of Representatives, then as a lobbyist downtown, kayaking gave me a reason to fail at my job. The river of politics still scared me, and there was no gauge to tell me when it would flood. I knew the level above which I would not paddle on the Potomac but did not yet know the political level above which I would not go. Constantly torn between my career and the river, I always chose the river. Whenever the gauge spiked, I would change my schedule, call in sick, and turn my back on Capitol Hill.

I thought of leaving Washington, but the river kept me there. I told myself I only needed one more hurricane before I could leave, satisfied that I had tamed my obsession. I was really waiting for my father to tell me that I had achieved enough in politics, that seeking a higher level might cost me everything.

Waiting for another hurricane required geologic patience. I prayed for a fat Category 5 to veer up the Atlantic Coast, west into the Chesapeake, and stall for a week. Instead, they sneaked into the Gulf, hiccupped across Florida, and skidded through the Carolinas. Before work, Stephen and I did pushups and situps and ran slalom gates on the Feeder Canal, dodging Canal Road traffic with our boats on our shoulders. We practiced with members of the U.S. kayak team, who would let us into their lineup and comment on our technique. This would have been the equivalent of meeting Tiger Woods at Hains Point and having him stop to give pointers. Often the air temperature was in the single digits, and the river gurgled like a polluted Slurpee. My life jacket would be so encrusted with ice that the zipper only thawed on my way home to change into a suit, while I listened to Bob Edwards on NPR.

As the level rose in my life as a lobbyist, I foolishly thought the tan lines on my wrists and neck spoke of my superior life as a riverman. Some of my colleagues concluded that I was a freak who lacked commitment. I should have been paying for the privilege of pheasant hunting on the Eastern Shore with Congressmen dressed like Orvis models, not jostling with gray people in vile polypropylene in a shuttle van along a gorge in West Virginia. I remember one impromptu meeting with my boss during which I expected to get fired and was instead given a bonus. I told myself the lie that the old rules didn't apply, that there was no longer a direct relationship between time and money. I rededicated myself to the Potomac River and started doing remarkably stupid things in my kayak.

A string of high-profile politicians fell from grace.

On the river, more kayakers were having close calls as the sport took off in popularity and young, bulletproof paddlers ran Great Falls in shiny boats. No longer was the river only claiming bank fishermen who slipped into the flood surge days after the rains had ended. Inevitably, someone died running Great Falls, sucked into Charlie's Hole, swallowed indifferently by chocolate milk. I was on the river the morning after, looking around each rock for the body. The ribs of a deer carcass gave me a fright.

I had a series of two-shirt days on Capitol Hill, suffering legislative losses and enduring the cell-phone wrath of clients who felt they were being baited and switched. In fact, I had two clients I loved and five that I did not, but couldn't see how to survive with only two. I was overextended, trying to be a K-Street lobbyist and a riverman. My reputation seemed to decline in direct relation to the amount of time I wanted to paddle, not whether I actually went paddling. The river became an escape from my self-loathing at the kind of lobbyist I had become.

Then Stephen and I confronted Hurricane Ivan, when 50,000 more cubic feet of water passed under our boats every second than pass over Niagara Falls—enough to fill the Reflecting Pool every four and a half seconds. Our luck did not hold. First, Stephen and his kayak rotated into a raging, pitchblend whirlpool. When he pulled off his spray skirt to escape, he and his boat disappeared. Ten. Fifteen. Twenty seconds later and 100 yards downstream, he reappeared, bluefaced. His boat shot lengthwise from the water, fell over, and floated by his side. He clung to it like Ishmael to Quoqueeq's coffin. I pulled him to shore, and he said flatly, "Don't pull your skirt. Die in your boat if you have to. At least we'll be able to find you."

Late the same afternoon I blindly ran a drop, flipped over into a brain freeze, opened my eyes, and freaked out. I broke my paddle on a rock as I missed my roll and wrenched my shoulder. I hung limply, defeated, oddly serene, staring into limitless black at 4 feet under. I thought, *I will stay with my boat, but Stephen will not be able to help me, and I will die.* The river filled my mouth, sinuses, eyes, and lungs.

My mother screamed. My father shook his head in pity and would not call the Park Service. My colleagues did not look up from their Blackberries. My wife worried alone at night then remarried. My children cried at the first Christmas, had a moment of silence at the second, grew up, married, and told stories about their crazy first father. Then, thirty years of muscle memory kicked in, and I rolled with half a paddle and scrounged to an eddy.

I stayed out of the boat for six months and discovered claustrophobia in an MRI machine while scanning a torn rotator cuff. I hated my job and hated myself for hating it but felt overpowered, with the current moving quickly, and the level rising. I stopped checking the river level, stopped reading the *Washington Post*. And, finally, I sold my kayak.

I NOW LIVE IN CALIFORNIA, where the sky is cloudless most of the year. I bought a surfboard, and a handful of locals let me share their break and make an ass of myself in knee-high waves. The fear I still crave comes from knowing that we are not the dominant predators in the ecosystem. The water is cold. My fingers stiffen so that later I can't turn the ignition. Bob Edwards is no longer there to thaw me on the way home.

Recently, I stood on a bridge over a local creek. I ran a mental line through an upstream drop, imagined myself eddying out behind a rock just above the bridge piling. I closed my eyes, listened to the roar of the water, and drew deeply the pungent stench of runoff. Richard Nixon, of course, then adrenaline as I imagined being dragged into a strainer of willow branches, the paddle stripped from my hands. Startled, I blinked open my eyes and pushed back from the railing. I turned to go, hoping my parents would approve of me abandoning rivers.

I am still a lobbyist. I did not tell my fourth-grade teacher this is what I would do, but I work very hard at it every day. The quality of my work has improved because I am genuinely flattered that my two clients retain me. I am also honest with them about being obsessed with my family and our outdoor life over more important, national issues. I am no longer afraid of drowning in politics, nor of being eaten by one of the dominant predators.

I fly back to Washington often, and as the plane follows the Shenandoah and banks east at Harper's Ferry, I see the Potomac River and miss it with an ache-like sexual hunger. But without the high-powered job, I no longer need the river as a mistress to console me for not reaching a high enough level.

STEVE WHITAKER has worked for over ten years for the U.S. Congress and as a lobbyist in Washington, D.C. He lives on the central coast of California with his family and teaches at Cal Poly and Johns Hopkins. He is the author of *Anarchist-Individualism and the Origins of Italian Fascism.*

WILLIAM KLOEFKORN

October

This leaf from that legacy maple is the color
of the fine expensive wine
six years ago
I gave up drinking,

and hanging from the limbs of another tree
are the amber hues of so many
many drafts and gills
so many nights ago
I said goodbye to.

Water over ice in a delicate glass
I rescued from my dead mother's kitchen.
Take it, she would have said, and
put it to good use.

I did. I lift it now to know its clarity.
Six years or ninety-one:
At the end of any stretch there
lies another. Here's to the stretch. Here's
to the end. Here's to whatever time
it takes to have the heart it takes
once more to get there.

See page 20 for this author's background information.

PART IV

The Big Ticket

At the end of any stretch there
lies another. Here's to the stretch. Here's
to the end. Here's to whatever time
it takes to have the heart it takes
once more to get there.

—WILLIAM KLOEFKORN, OCTOBER (p. 115)
See also *Secrets of Heaven* 6–13, Swedenborg (pp. 161–162).

Daffodils

For weeks after Lana's funeral,
my mother cooked for me,
handled death's paperwork,
opened a door—
Look outside at your backyard.
Looking outward for the first time since burial
prayers, I saw daffodils blooming,
the ones that Lana and I had planted
in a sunken rectangular spot last fall,
set against the bright, new green of spring,
Easter white and careless yellow.

TOM LOMBARDO's poems have appeared in *Oxford American, Southern Poetry Review, New York Quarterly, Hampden-Sydney Poetry Review, Pearl, Poet Lore, Hawai'i Review, Orbis: Quarterly International Literary Journal,* and many others. He holds a master's degree in fine arts from Queens University of Charlotte, a master's degree in journalism from Ohio University, and a bachelor's degree in metallurgical engineering from Carnegie–Mellon University. He teaches creative writing at the Savannah College of Art and Design, Atlanta.

FRANZ DOUSKEY

Wake Up in Glory

MY BROTHER TAL SAID THAT WHEN HE DIED he would give me a sign. Once, when he was near death, he saw a hyper-white light at the end of a tunnel. He wanted to get nearer to it. As he moved toward the light, the light dimmed, and when he opened his eyes, he saw doctors and nurses, the bright operating-room lights ricocheting off everything stainless steel. It hurt his eyes when he tried to keep them open, so he closed them and woke up again in post-op, unaware that he had died on the operating table. He had crossed over to the other side for about twenty minutes before his heart could be restarted. Maybe it affected his brain. I don't know. But after that, Tal was always talking about that unearthly light, how beautiful it was, and how he could see the walls of heaven, and ghostly figures, maybe angels, and someone, a faded creature who looked like our younger brother Jack who was killed by an overloaded poultry truck. It was tottering from side to side while Jack lazily rode his bike back and forth on the dirt road in front of our farmhouse.

The night before Tal died, I had the sweats, needed a blanket, and I even put on flannel pajama bottoms because my legs were so cold. It was July, a hot and humid night in Monroe, Louisiana. I looked at the outdoor digital thermometer. It read 84 degrees at two in the morning. Just after nine o'clock I got a call from Tal's son, Dusty, that Tal had gone. The night sweats was not the sign I was expecting.

Tal's wife, Laura, had died in May. That was quite a shock. She was in good health, but one night she felt tired, had a terrible headache, and then she was gone. We thought Tal would go first because he had been so sick with diabetes, a chronic cough from years of smoking, and a number of bouts with pneumonia almost every winter.

After the last operation, Tal talked about dying, that he was looking forward to it so he could see our parents again. He made it sound as though there was a constant party going on in heaven, where people were reunited with ones who had gone before. I wish I had that kind of belief.

Tal said, "When I get there, I will see Jack again and all my friends."

"How are you going to recognize them, and how are they going to recognize you?" I reasoned, "You're going to be dust."

"The hell I am. Whatever is there will be recognized, which is why I'm not going to be cremated. I don't want to make the resurrection any harder than it's supposed to be."

"But supposing you get killed when an oil tanker crashes into your car and explodes into flames. You're body won't last a second. All that's going to be left is a greasy cinder in the middle of the road," I said.

"It doesn't take a second for your soul to rise. There is no time in heaven. There is no time here, only light," Tal explained. "Time is just something you put on a wall."

"But Tal, supposing you don't believe that. I can't believe that."

"Well, T.C., it don't matter what you think or what you believe because someone's faith or lack of faith does not cause one ripple in the universe. It is the light of this world, and that light is the light out of this world."

There was no sense of arguing with him. Even if you happened to ask him how the crops were doing, eventually Tal would talk about vibrations and auras and synergies, and we all began to think that there was something not right about the boy.

After Laura's death Tal started going downhill. They had worked hard and kept the farm going when everyone around them was selling out to developers. They raised four children, two boys and two girls, out of that soil. They taught them right. Tal's children were the first in our family to go to college. After that they had families of their own, moved away, and came back home less and less.

They all showed up for Laura's funeral, and when it was over, a few of the children tried to convince Tal that he should give up the farm and move in with them. He wouldn't hear of it. He said he would be fine and that he had a lot of work to do because things have a way of falling into disrepair so easily. But two months later Tal was gone.

When Tal's children arrived with their children, we gathered at the old farmhouse, hugged and cried, and wandered around the place looking for familiar things to give us comfort. My wife, Kathleen,

stayed away. Tal had scared her during his final months, and she didn't like to go back to the old house. She thought someone had put a spell on him or at the very least had given Tal the evil eye.

IT WAS HOT AND HUMID, and we didn't want to take too much time to decide what kind of service to have for Tal. A few of his children said cremation would be the best thing, quick and inexpensive, but I told them about Tal's feelings. I said that I knew what Tal would want, and that they should decide on the hymns, and I'll take care of things with McGimsey, the undertaker. We were too tired to discuss it for very long. Maybe it was the heat and humidity, the shock of losing Laura so unexpectedly, and then Tal going so soon after.

The children decided on *(There'll Be) Peace in the Valley, Amazing Grace,* and *When I Wake Up in Glory.* I added *Swing Down, Chariot,* which was one of Tal's favorites. I took care of buying the coffin— brass with fluted corners and a raised, diagonal cross across the divided coffin lid. I picked out the blue suit from the three in Tal's closet, along with a fairly new white shirt and a bright royal blue tie with little white sailboats on it. I brought the clothes to Barney McGimsey.

McGimsey had taken care of my parents' and Laura's funerals. He wanted to bury Tal in some official undertaker clothes, you know, the jacket and shirt with no back so you could slip them over a stiff body easier than with regular clothing. But I put Tal's clothes in McGimsey's hands and said, "I want my brother to look like himself. His own clothes will do fine."

Before I left McGimsey, I gave him some special instructions to take care of before Tal's waking hours the next day. At first, McGimsey scratched his head and said he wasn't sure, but then I handed him an extra twenty dollar bill and that seemed to clear things up for him.

The next afternoon just before four, my wife, Tal's children and grandchildren, and I gathered at McGimsey's Funeral Home. We spoke in hushed monosyllables and watched as the parking lot began to fill, then back up into the street, causing a traffic jam. I guess people wanted to say goodbye. After all, Tal had lived here all his life. He was a good man and had done a lot of good.

We filed into the room where Tal's coffin was surrounded by rows and rows of flowers and dozens of family photographs. I walked up to the open coffin and peered inside before I offered a few words to the crowd that had filled the pink-lit room. I said that my words would be brief, that Tal believed in a better place, and that he was ready to leave his body and go forward to what he always described as that bright unearthly light. This wasn't a time to grieve because Tal is someone who believed in the power of the Lord, and that he would finally walk into that powerful light and see once again all those people he had loved who had gone before. "So friends and family, when you see Tal for the last time, rejoice. He has gone to that great light."

I moved away from the coffin. People slowly began to approach the bier. First, his children, grandchildren, then his friends. They saw that Tal was ready to meet his Heavenly Maker. He looked terrific. When people peered into the satin-lined coffin, some gasped, others smiled. My wife gave me one of her looks. They saw Tal, his face fixed in a smile, wearing the blue suit, the white shirt, and the royal blue tie with the little white sailboats. Tal was lying in state, all dressed up with only one place to go. I saw to it that Tal was wearing a large pair of stylish Ban-Rays to make that final, great hyper-white light easier on his eyes. He wouldn't have to blink or turn away but could watch it coming at him, that *thank God Almighty light of this world*, leading to the other world, surrounding him, lifting him up and taking him home.

FRANK DOUSKEY's writing has appeared in the *Nation, Rolling Stone, Yankee, Down East, The New Yorker,* and *Callaloo.* He is working on a book titled, "A Wild Indolence Has Taken Me This Far," but it seems to be taking forever to finish.

VIRGIL SUÁREZ

Recitative after G. de Chirico's "Les adieux éternels"

We are burying my father-in-law in the cemetery
on Calle Ocho in Miami, the one with the Cuban
flags, the mausoleum of ten-thousand martyrs

dead. The flowers spike the ground everywhere;
we weave among them, mortals awaiting the song
of the rooster. The sun glares off the pink roses,

the meaty ones paled by so much light; we walk
silent enshrouded in shadow. We are pallbearers,
my father-in-law's bones speak through the creaks

of the casket. Fernando, the man next to me, best
friend to the deceased cannot control himself so he
begins to hum Carlos Gardel's famous song: *"Adíos*

muchachos compañeros de mi vida . . ." The gaping
wound of earth awaits this body, and the next.
Flowering of the living, of the dying. In this light

a rose propped against so much marble shimmers,
glows in the afternoon light like a torch, a beacon.
We carry on, ready to accept we are one with roses.

VIRGIL SUÁREZ is the author of most recently *90 Miles: New and Selected*, published by the University of Pittsburgh Press. He teaches at Bennington College and Florida State University. Currently, he is working on a book of photopoems.

SYLVIA M. SHAW

The Realist and the Dreamer

A MAN WHO CAN TRANSFORM A NEW ENGLAND LAKE INTO A RIVER of the Mexican tropics has lived in my thoughts as long as I can remember, even to those earliest memories—only part experience, part dream—Abuelito, my Mexican grandfather, José Tamborrel.

Although he is dead, he continues to challenge my illusory sense of independence, of separateness. I didn't know this when I penciled my first letters to him at age eight; I knew it even less in my adolescence or in my newlywed years when I still walked about the planet as if I were miraculously sprung out of nothingness into full-blown everythingness. In college I puzzled over Swedenborg's concept that all thoughts flow into us from spirit, that nothing is truly our own. As an aspiring novelist, I rejected such a notion and filled reams of paper with utterly unique ideas.

Asher Brown Durand.
A River Landscape.
Oil on canvas,
32 x 48 in., 1858.
Fine Arts Museums
of San Francisco.
Gift of Mr. and Mrs. John
D. Rockefeller III.

Somewhere between my Mexican childhood and American adulthood, somewhere between reality and perception, I have come to understand Swedenborg's concept of humanness as a paradox. For me, to be human is to be both empty vessel and creator, passive receptor and active force. I see myself as a recipient of ideas formulated long before. Nothing is new. Yet all is new. I am only the conglomerate of genetic material and environment; nevertheless, I am unique, creating myself with every breath.

Whether truth be paradoxical or not, in the calm darkness of a New England lake, I come back to my grandfather with stubborn insistence—a mountain, a fixed point in my landscape, even now when we no longer inhabit the same world. How often, when I trek through Massachusetts snow, do I remember the ivy-clothed palm trees of the garden he designed. I hear him—Mexican scholar and businessman—through the unlikeliest sounds: in the calm of Rachmaninoff's *Variations on a Theme by Corelli*, in the allegro of August crickets, in the deep roar of a jet challenging earth and sky. I see him in my aesthetic drive to transcend the commonplace: even in the woodwork of my house which wouldn't meet his standards. Dents and children's fingerprints draw him to me in silent, smiling admonition: *you need to wash and paint your house, Sylvia.*

Seven summers after his death, my grandfather transforms a moonlit lake in Massachusetts into the Usumacinta of tropical Tabasco. The full moon cuts a path from the darkened shore to me in the anchored boat. Tonight there is no lake, only a river I never saw in the jungles of Tabasco where he tried to make the family fortune, a boy of fourteen. Fatherless. A mother and four sisters to support. The Revolution, eating its way into the Mexican soul and body, consuming flesh and idealism alike. The Tamborrel family had lost everything, except for two parcels of land in the Mexican tropics.

Young and ambitious, my grandfather resolved to claim and work his inheritance. He, a streetwise kid of fourteen, would hire a band of Tabascan men to go with him into the jungle for six months to harvest chicle, an audacious plan. Who in his right mind would finance such a scheme? Yet there was one—a businessman. What did he see in the boy's eyes that made him believe he would see a full return with profit? Whatever he saw, he financed the project.

The city boy traveled the Usumacinta River and watched the moon as I do now. He harvested the chicle, paid his debts, and left Tabasco with ten thousand pesos in gold. But he failed to recognize human greed and chicanery. In one night he lost all his earnings to professional gamblers on a riverboat.

"I staggered to the deck," my grandfather told me. "It was night. A bright moon lit up the river. A breeze blew. But I could hardly breathe. I struggled to the stern and climbed over the railing. I could hear the water churning. I wanted to drown myself. Anything but go home empty-handed! Anything but admit how stupid, stupid I was! Then I thought of my mother, how lost she would be, and I couldn't do it. I couldn't do that to her. So I went home in defeat and humiliation, as poor as the day I had left—and started again."

A decade later my grandfather established a successful import and export company that allowed him eventually to immerse himself in two passions: study and philanthropy. Although he left school at age nine, he became a most literate man. He had a photographic memory that was a marvel and clear-sightedness that never left him, even in the end when cancer had savaged his body. He was a realist's realist. Yet his *objets d'art*, like his house, his life itself, betrayed a romantic spirit. The paradoxical man—realist and dreamer.

Only now in middle life do I recognize that duality in myself. He labored over twenty years to write an encyclopedia single-handedly! Was that any less foolish, any less a colossal task than mine to write the definitive saga of the Mexican Revolution? His volumes, thirty or more of them, stand in silent dusty rows as do all four versions and twenty odd years of my own magnum opus. Testaments in futility.

I enter his study and pull out the R volume of his unfinished encyclopedia. My finger digs a canal through the dust. I can sense the family's collective shrug: what wasted effort! But I blow off the dust, fine as the powdered scales of a butterfly's wing, and know the hours, the days, the years charted with silent, intense activity. I remember nights when the world sleeps and the writer travels alone through that inner landscape familiar and unfamiliar, wondrous and frightening, erotic and bland, colorful and colorless. I know firsthand the writer's plea, charged with deep longing. It is the acknowledgement, fatalistic as Tristan and Isolde's decision to face damnation rather than renounce their love, ambitious and hell-bent as Faust's pact with the devil, noble as Milton in all his blindness:

Lord! Take anything away but my ability to think, to link words!

In Abuelito's silent study, I pick up a leather-bound copy of his memoirs. As I read, I know only too well what the process of writing them gave him. Later, back in Massachusetts trolling dark water, gazing at a full moon, I transform a lake into a river. Something else my grandfather's life taught me: that success and failure are the top and bottom side of a wing in flight. Despair is carried upward by joy; joy downward by despair. Both act that we may fly.

I saw José Tamborrel's despair in 1984 after cancer had launched its insidious attack. Despair ambushed him the day after my sister's wedding. Despite his pain, he had overseen the preparations, making sure the house was clean, silver polished, garden paths swept to perfection, the marble statues washed, and that a huge white canopy transformed the garden by the pool into a sanctuary for the ceremony. The house and gardens filled with guests. Mexican relatives mingled easily with the exuberant foreigners. My grandfather greeted them all. During the reception, while everyone danced, he withdrew to his study. It was a beautiful wedding. Then it was over.

The next day, as the umbrella tables and the dance floor were dismantled, I went into the study to say goodbye as I had done all my life. Always goodbye to this man, this second father of mine. Always hundreds of miles muscling between us. At the critical moment as I kissed him, he clutched my hand and shut his eyes tightly. Tears slipped past the lidded sentries. His shoulders shook as he sobbed his despair over the cancer's newest indignity of incontinence and pain.

"I can't take this anymore! Not this!" he cried.

I hugged him and let him cry. When he could talk, he pulled away. Still holding my hand, he muttered in staccato words, "I tried to kill myself last night. I put the gun to my head. I kept thinking, I could pull the trigger and make this all stop now before it gets worse. Then I thought about my head, shattered by the bullet, and I started to think about your grandmother or one of the children walking in here and finding me! I thought about the police! My God! I can't even kill myself! They've taken that away from me too!"

Now I was crying, kissing his hand. "Please don't ever think of doing such a thing! We all need you!" And then I found myself conceding, out of fairness, out of love for him, "At least, don't do it yet. Not yet. Give yourself time to make sure things are really permanently worse. It's still too soon. Things could change for the better. . . ."

On the flight home, I gazed at an expanse of clouds, thick as snowdrifts. I could not condemn his attempted suicide. Who am I, in my healthy body, to judge him? I am not on the rack.

We make choices all our lives. Isn't free will the very hallmark of our humanity? It strikes me that self-deliverance from the rack is one more choice, rendered good or evil by the motive more than by the deed itself. The motives behind a suicide are as censurable or as commendable as the broad spectrum of human motivation. We shudder at a young person who takes his own life as a way of punishing his parents. We applaud a soldier's selflessness when he deliberately throws himself on a live grenade in order to save his comrades.

Society tends to be less sympathetic when the motive for suicide is deliverance from extreme pain. If a house is on fire, is it wrong to open the door and escape the horror of the flames? How is it different if it's your body that is on fire with a terminal disease, and you believe the door opens to eternal life?

The plane streaked across the sky. I gazed into the strange white landscape, the one that always makes me most keenly aware of the presence of God, perhaps because it is so extraordinary to have a bird's-eye view of the world, or because I am moved by the beauty of clouds and sky seen from above, or because no matter how often I fly, I am still awed by the mystery of flight. For all of these reasons and more, I found myself praying into the vastness outside my window:

Oh, Lord, help us to do your will, to live useful lives. Grant us the courage to face whatever we must and to endure, if by enduring we serve your purposes. But if our courage fails us, at least grant us the wisdom to know when our lives have truly reached the point of no return. Forgive us if we err in our judgment; the flames are so painful.

In the end, my grandfather did not commit suicide. He was the same fourteen-year-old boy who could not bring himself to take his own life. Cowardice? Duty? Perhaps both. Our instinct for preservation is born out of fear. Fear is a powerful motivator. So, too, is love. To live with pain and uncertainty takes courage. There is also the issue of timing. In 1984, it simply wasn't my grandfather's time anymore than in 1917. I know that because one Saturday, several months after the wedding, he phoned me from Mexico City, his voice vibrant.

"Sylvita!" he called me by my nickname. "I feel so good! Everything is so much better!"

He spoke with the voice of a young man. I still wonder at it. He had been granted a boon, a respite in the long battle.

Four years later it finally overtook him, when he was too sick to take matters into his own hands. The hospitalization daily chipped away at his dignity. Death was long and painful. Assisted suicide would have spared him much suffering at that point. Mercifully, he finally slipped into a coma. Children and grandchildren kept vigil, flinching at the raspiness of his breath, marveling at how his heart kept beating with stubborn insistence as the rest of his body shut down.

I was unable to travel to Mexico, so I said goodbye to José Tamborrel at the lake. Swimming into the late afternoon sun, I spoke to him across shimmering miles. And I felt him near on that last day. That is the chief paradox of them all. I think of that voice on the phone, so strangely young at the very time when he was old and emaciated. I think of him dead and not dead. Wasted and invigorated. Asleep and waking into a light that is new, yet known all along.

SYLVIA M. SHAW is a professor of rhetoric at Boston University. She is currently writing a mystery novel and a screenplay. Both are set in the Mexican Revolution of 1910 and reflect in different ways the duality of her heritage as a Mexican American.

LOUIS E. BOURGEOIS

Leaving

The house has never
been so dark.
I don't turn the lights on,
I can't take the light.

A pair of faded stilettos
in the closet,
a strand of brown
hair in the bathroom sink.
Your favorite white cup,
still on the counter.

The house has always
been this bright.
I can't stand the sun;
the windows are nailed up
with old wood.

I keep hearing whispers, Cora.
The back door won't go silent,

and pigeons fly
in and out of the eaves
as if nothing has happened.

LOUIS E. BOURGEOIS lives on a farm in north Mississippi. His latest collection of poems, *OLGA*, was released in 2005 by WordTech. Currently, he is working on a collection of stories entitled *The Gar Diaries*.

Swedenborg's Inner Journey

SWEDENBORG was born in a home that would provide him with a firm foundation for his spiritual researches. His father, Jesper Swedberg (1653–1735), was a pastor of solid and simple convictions in a Sweden dominated by the Lutheran state church. Alarmed by the complacency of his fellow Swedes, which he ascribed to solifidism, the doctrine of justification by faith alone, Swedberg denounced what he called "faith of the head" and insisted that true Christianity must be lived out in practice. Jesper Swedberg was a commanding presence. His energy and uprightness enabled him to rise in his profession: he was made bishop of Skara in 1702, a position he would hold until his death in 1735.

Emanuel Swedenborg was born in Stockholm on January 29, 1688, the third child and second son of Swedberg and his wife, Sara Behm (1666–1696), daughter of a wealthy mine owner. Little is known of Swedenborg's early life, but he retrospectively provides a glimpse of his youthful religious experience in a letter written in 1769 in which he describes being constantly engaged in thought about God at ages four to ten and later about his delight as a youth in talking with clergymen about faith. Swedenborg's diary of his spiritual experiences, written in his late middle age, suggests a link between his early and later spiritual life. He observed a close connection between rhythms of breathing and states of consciousness, and he remarks that even in his childhood he was accustomed to holding his breath in prayer and to coordinate his breathing with his heartbeat. When he did, he noticed that "his intellectual capacity would often begin to

virtually disappear." Similarly, when as a mature man he was engaged in writing in a state of inspiration, he would find that his breath would almost stop. It is interesting to note that regulation and cessation of breath is often associated with mystical experiences. One Buddhist sutra says the Buddha's breath ceased for six years as he meditated before reaching enlightenment.

In 1699, at the age of eleven, Swedenborg matriculated at the University of Uppsala, where his father was then a professor. Although the university's ledger describes Swedenborg as "a youth of the best talent," early matriculation was not such an indication of precocity as it may appear: universities at the time provided something akin to secondary education. Already well versed in Latin, the common language of European scholarship in which all his major works would be written, Swedenborg enrolled in the faculty of philosophy, a curriculum that included science and mathematics. In 1702, Jesper Swedberg moved his family from Uppsala to take up his bishopric at Skara. Emanuel was left behind with his older sister Anna (1686–1766), who had married the distinguished humanist Erik Benzelius (1675–1743), the university's librarian. Swedenborg would live with the Benzelius family for the rest of his student years. The relationship between Swedenborg and Benzelius was to become a warm one, and much of Swedenborg's early correspondence is addressed to his brother-in-law.

In 1709, Swedenborg presented his thesis, a commentary on some maxims from Latin authors. The presentation of his thesis was to mark the end of his formal education. In that era it was customary for young men of Swedenborg's class to take an extensive tour of Europe upon completing their studies. It was intended that he should go to England, the world's center of scientific learning at that time, but he was forced by political circumstances to delay this trip. There was the disastrous defeat of Sweden's King Charles XII (1682–1718) by the armies of the Russian czar Peter the Great (1672–1725) at Poltava in 1709. The Danes, who were also at war with Sweden, dominated the seas, making passage to England almost impossible.

Several months of enforced and unwelcome leisure led Swedenborg to apply to study as a private pupil of Christopher Polhem (1661–1751), the most respected inventor in Sweden. Although Polhem would become another influence on Swedenborg's early life, their meeting was delayed for several years by Swedenborg's decision to take a ship leaving for England in the summer of 1710.

Once safely in London, Swedenborg plunged into the current ferment of science and technology. He frequented a circle that included such luminaries as Isaac Newton (1642–1727) and Edmond Halley (1656–1742) and lodged with artisans of various trades to learn their

Opposite:
Boardman Robinson.
Judson Stannard.
Gouache on masonite,
14.8 x 11.92 in.,
ca. 1944.
Collection of The
University of Arizona
Museum of Art, Tucson.
Gift of C. Leonard
Pfeiffer.

crafts. He also became friendly with John Flamsteed (1646–1719), the brilliant but cantankerous Astronomer Royal, for whom Greenwich Observatory was built. Swedenborg managed to disarm Flamsteed's suspicions and spent a great deal of time with him, observing his methods and instruments, reporting on them to Swedish scientists in Uppsala, and working on the leading scientific question of the time: finding the correct longitude at sea.

Swedenborg spent two-and-a-half years in England before moving on to the Netherlands and France to continue his scientific investigations. He turned his mind to inventions of all sorts, and in a 1714 letter to Erik Benzelius, he boasts of having plans for inventions including a submarine, an air gun that could fire a thousand shots at once, and "a universal musical instrument, whereby the most inexperienced player can produce all kinds of melodies, these being found marked on paper and in notes." He sent these plans home, but on his return to Sweden at the end of 1714, he found that his father had unfortunately mislaid them. They have never been recovered.

OVERALL SWEDENBORG'S FIRST YEAR AT HOME was one of frustration. He found no professional post. Indeed the only project that bore fruit at this time was the *Daedalus Hyperboreus (Northern Daedalus)*, a scientific journal Swedenborg had undertaken to publish. Six issues of this periodical would appear between 1716 and 1718. The title *Daedalus* was chosen as a compliment to Polhem, and the issues contained a number of Polhem's articles and designs. Upon returning to his homeland, Swedenborg had fulfilled his ambition of several years earlier and made friends with the distinguished inventor, serving for some time as his assistant. The publication met with the approval of Charles XII, who was extremely interested in science and technology, and in late 1716 Swedenborg, in the company of Polhem, made the monarch's acquaintance. The king soon became a powerful sponsor of Swedenborg. At Polhem's behest, the king offered the young man a choice of three posts. Swedenborg chose the position of assessor extraordinary at the Bergscollegium, or Board of Mines, not only because of his family connections to the mining industry but because it offered him the greatest chance of scientific investigation. The mining industry had the only laboratories and workshops in Sweden at that time.

IN 1719 ULRIKA ELEONORA (1688–1741), the sister of Charles XII, ascended to the throne as queen. In May of that year the Swedberg family was ennobled and given the surname by which Emanuel has come to be known—not in consequence of his own achievements but be-

cause the queen hoped the Swedbergs and other families similarly ennobled would form a supportive faction in the nobility.

Despite his rise in status, this was a time of setbacks for
Swedenborg. The death of Charles XII, his royal patron, enabled the
Board of Mines to eliminate Swedenborg's salary and to keep him
from being appointed as a full assessor. Although he persistently promoted his own case, he did not succeed in getting a full appointment
and salary until 1724.

The year 1720 was marked by the death of Swedenborg's step-
mother, and his inheritance from her eventually provided him with
financial security at a time when he had no job. Swedenborg took another trip abroad that lasted from May 1720 to July 1722. During this
time he visited the Netherlands and Germany to gather information
about mining. On his return, he devoted himself to writing about
mining, metallurgy, and finance. In 1724, he received his long-await-
ed full appointment to the Board of Mines, on which he would serve
for the next twenty-five years.

IN 1728, SWEDENBORG, by now settled in a house of his own in
Stockholm, resumed his literary activities, which had been interrupt-
ed by more commonplace duties. He began to write his three-volume
*Opera Philosophica et Mineralia (Philosophical and Metallurgical
Works)*, which would take him five years to complete and which he
would publish in 1734. The first volume, titled the *Principia Rerum
Naturalium (Basic Principles of Nature)*, constitutes his first major
philosophical work. Along with *De Infinito (The Infinite)*, also published in 1734, it provides the most comprehensive portrait of
Swedenborg's philosophical thought before his visionary experiences
began in earnest.

In these works, three things stand out as especially noteworthy.
The first is Swedenborg's effort to reason deductively, from first principles, as well as empirically, from evidence: he contends that both are
equally important. This concern reflects one of the great philosophical issues of his era: the relationship between knowledge *a priori*
(which explains phenomena by a system built up from one's initial
intellectual principles) and knowledge *a posteriori* (which is inferred
from observed phenomena). The discussion of these different types
of knowledge would reach its culmination in the major work of
German philosopher Immanuel Kant (1724–1804), *Critique of Pure
Reason* (1781). The second is Swedenborg's concern to relate the infinite to the finite. His means of doing so is by positing the mathe-
matical point, the juncture between the infinite and the finite, as the
basis of all manifest reality: "It is comparable to the two-faced Janus,

seeing in opposite directions simultaneously, each of his two faces turned toward one of the two universes."

The third, and perhaps most distinctive, aspect of this phase of Swedenborg's work is that he accepts the mechanistic worldview of the era, but only to a degree. In *Basic Principles of Nature* he writes: "The world is mechanical and consists of a series of finite things, which have resulted from the most varied contingencies; ... the world can accordingly be investigated by experience and with the aid of geometry." But, as he goes on to say, "the infinite cannot be comprehended by geometry," nor can the "mental principle in the soul." Swedenborg asks, "What is this something in the soul, which is nothing mechanical, and what are the appropriate means of understanding it?" Even at this comparatively early stage of his thought, he is drawn away from purely scientific investigations toward a deeper level of knowledge.

LIKE MOST OF SWEDENBORG S WRITINGS, *Basic Principles of Nature* was published abroad—in this case, in Dresden and Leipzig. At this point Swedenborg settled into a pattern that would become standard for the rest of his life. He would spend some time in his native country, then would depart for extended trips abroad, sometimes lasting three or four years, to England or the European continent, where he would publish one or more of his books. This particular journey, lasting from May 1733 to July 1734, took him to Germany and Bohemia.

When Swedenborg returned to Sweden in 1734, he found it in political crisis. There was much agitation for war with Russia to regain the territories Sweden had lost under Charles XII. As a member of the House of Nobles, he drafted a memorandum opposing war on the grounds that the risks far outweighed any likely gains and that "Russia is indeed more formidable than before."

In July 1736, Swedenborg set out for another trip, which would take him to Rome via Paris, Venice, and Bologna. En route he stopped in Amsterdam, where he began to write his next major work, the *Oeconomia Regni Animalis (Dynamics of the Soul's Domain)*. The first volume, completed in 1739 and anonymously published in 1740, mainly discusses the heart and the blood, which, Swedenborg said, are "the complex of all things that exist in the world and the storehouse ... of all that exists in the body." The second volume, published in 1741, covers the brain, the nervous system, and the soul.

In this work Swedenborg describes an intricate interrelation among the blood, the cerebrospinal fluid, and the "spirituous fluid," a subtle substance that constitutes the essence of life. He also sets out a view of the structure of the human soul, which, he argues, consists of a higher, intuitive, spiritual faculty called the *anima;* the familiar rational mind, or *mens;* and the so-called vegetative soul, or *animus,* which controls vital functions. In a portrait that echoes his later vision of the human soul as a meeting place between the contending forces of hell and heaven, he describes the *mens* as divided between the higher, heavenly impulses of the *anima,* and the coarse physical urges of the *animus.* The *mens* is, thus, the battleground on which the struggle of human free will is played out.

SWEDENBORG'S PROJECT OF EXPLORING the entirety of the human body as a vehicle for the soul was interrupted by a radical change in his life's direction. It was to mark the turning point in his life, and it would lead him to the vocation for which he would be most remembered—that of spiritual visionary and sage.

The process was a slow one. Although a devout Christian all his life, Swedenborg had not made religious issues per se the primary subject of his writing. Instead he had attempted to explore such questions as infinity and the nature of the soul primarily through scientific methods. The cleft between science and religion was not as great in his day as it is in ours. Even at this stage, his views tended toward what scholars today would consider an esoteric perspective, though some of his readers might reject that classification. His notion of the *anima* as set out in *Dynamics of the Soul's Domain,* with its intuitive, higher perception of truth, illustrates this tendency.

Moreover, this transition in Swedenborg's intellectual thought appears to have been the result of his own inner experience. We have already seen how he learned to regulate his psychological state through breath control. While writing *Dynamics of the Soul's Domain,* he again observed how his breath would spontaneously cease when he was contemplating certain matters. He also referred to researchers whose conjectures were affirmed by "a certain cheering light, and joyful confirmatory brightness, . . . a kind of mysterious radiation—I know not whence it proceeds—that darts through some sacred temple of the brain." Scholars have naturally drawn from this reference the inference that he is speaking of his own experience.

Although Swedenborg would later say that his spiritual sight had been opened only in 1745, these early experiences suggest that this shift began several years before, around 1736. Possibly the death of his father the previous year turned his thoughts toward the Last Things. At any rate he began to record his dreams and spiritual experiences at this point. Unfortunately, this part of the biographical record is missing.

During these years, Swedenborg probably showed few, if any, outward signs of these shifts in his inner orientation: he continued to travel and work on his books as before. When he returned to

Sweden in 1740, he was elected to the newly established Academy of Sciences, an organization whose founding he had urged early in his own career. He resumed work at the Board of Mines and bought a house and garden in south Stockholm in March 1743, although he would not move there until three years later. He left Sweden again in July 1743 to complete and oversee the publication of *The Soul's Domain* in the Netherlands.

It was on this trip that the major events of his spiritual conversion took place, a conversion that would bring about great inner upheaval and transformation. We have an intimate portrait of one phase of this process in Swedenborg's *Journal of Dreams,* which recounts his inner experiences from March to October 1744. These records, intimate and often brutally frank, were not published in his lifetime and were never meant for publication. Despite, or because of this fact, they give us a tremendous amount of insight into this climactic moment in Swedenborg's life. Here we see classic elements of a religious conversion combined with highly personal details. At other times, he struggles between the worldly knowledge that has been his chief preoccupation up to that point and a higher, more spiritual knowledge.

In recent years psychiatrists have come to recognize the "spiritual emergency" as a unique psychological category. Although the process by which such "emergencies" occur is not well understood, they are common enough. In Christian contexts, as in Swedenborg's case, they can take the form of intense conversion experiences.

It was in the following spring that Swedenborg's orientation changed definitely and permanently: later he would say that this was the time when his spiritual eyes were opened. The incident occurred in April 1745. Swedenborg, dining alone in a private room in a London inn, saw and heard a man or an angel telling him not to eat too much. Then he saw a vapor rising from his body; it settled on the carpet and turned into worms of various types, which burned up with a loud pop. "A fiery light then appeared there and a rustling was audible," Swedenborg writes. "It felt as if all the worms produced by an immoderate appetite had been expelled and burnt, and I had been purged of them."

In July 1745, Swedenborg returned to his native country and resumed work on the Board of Mines. In the spring of the following year, he moved into the house he had bought three years earlier, which was located in the southern part of Stockholm. All the while he immersed himself in biblical exegesis according to the new understanding awakened by his spiritual sight. He began by preparing a three-volume Bible index for his own use and proceeded to write some smaller works.

During this time, Swedenborg seems to have been able to maintain a connection with the newly discovered spiritual world while in ordinary human company. "I mingled with others just as before," he writes, "and no one observed the fact that there was with me such a heavenly intercourse. In the midst of company I have sometimes spoken with spirits and with those who were around me.... At such times they could think no otherwise than that I was occupied with my thoughts."

HE ALSO KEPT UP HIS DUTIES WITH THE BOARD OF MINES, and when the post of councillor (a higher position than assessor, which was Swedenborg's title) became vacant, Swedenborg was offered the position. He not only declined, but, in order to devote all his time to his spiritual studies, he petitioned the king to relieve him of his duties and give him a pension equal to half his salary. His request was granted, and, in June 1747, Swedenborg took leave of the institution he had served for over thirty years. His intention was to devote his time to an exegesis of scripture. This work eventually took up three folio volumes in manuscript; nevertheless, it remained unfinished, and Swedenborg never published it.

Most likely Swedenborg changed his mind about this project because he felt it did not give a fully accurate portrayal of the unseen realities he had begun to encounter. Although the great turning point of Swedenborg's life and vision had come in 1744–1745, it appears that even after this time he did not understand the full spiritual sense of the scriptures. At least that was his own assessment.

By August 1747, however, he makes a note saying, "There was a change of state in me into the heavenly kingdom, in an image." Some of his followers have interpreted this as meaning that at this point his intuition was fully awakened to the deepest and most spiritual sense of scripture. He himself pointed out that *The Old Testament Explained* contained "the interior historical sense" of Genesis and Exodus, but not the deepest, spiritual sense. His magnum opus, *Arcana Coelestia (Secrets of Heaven)*, begun in December 1748, sets out his version of this spiritual sense. No longer do the stories of the Pentateuch merely serve as types for the coming Christian Church, but they apply to the inner life of the individual. The creation account of Genesis, for example, is seen in *Secrets of Heaven* 6–52 as a description of the regeneration of a human being: it begins in a dark state that is "without form and void" (Genesis 1:2) and reaches its conclusion—the fulfillment of spiritual potentiality—in the creation of a human being, "the image and likeness of God" (Genesis 1:26–27).

Hidden meanings in scripture—even several hidden meanings, each nested inside the other—have been a recurrent theme in the

Christian tradition from its beginnings. The earliest examples of allegorical exegesis of scripture appear in Philo of Alexandria, a Jewish philosopher who lived at the time of Christ. Following Philo's lead, the church father Origen (about 185 to about 254) taught that there were three senses of scripture, corresponding to the spirit, soul, and body (the tripartite structure of the human being as understood in early Christianity). In medieval times this was expanded to four different levels of meaning (expounded, for example, by Dante [1265–1321] in his Letter to Can Grande. The four-part structure was also adopted by the Jewish Kabbalists, who equated them with the four worlds of Kabbalistic teaching: the physical, psychological, spiritual, and divine. These ideas were in turn reabsorbed into esoteric Christianity. Swedenborg, too, saw three levels of meaning in scripture besides the literal.

These considerations lead to what may be the most vexed issue in Swedenborgian scholarship: How did Swedenborg's ideas relate to the esoteric and mystical currents of his era, as well as to broader trends in philosophical and theological thought?

Swedenborg himself stressed that his teachings were not influenced by human thought. He denied reading works of systematic theology both before and after his conversion, insisted on his total unfamiliarity with the works of the mystic Jacob Boehme (1575–1624), and condemned the Pietist mystic Johann Konrad Dippel (1678–1734). On the other hand, he must have had at least some familiarity with Philo's works—of which, as we have seen, Benzelius had prepared an edition—and his own library contained a number of works on esoteric topics such as magic, alchemy, and occultism.

As often happens, the most sensible conclusion seems to lie in a middle ground. It is unlikely that Swedenborg's exegesis had no connection with esoteric interpretations of the Bible prior to his own; on the other hand, that does not mean it was derivative of them. Swedenborg certainly had some ideas of the esoteric currents of his time; he is just as likely to have known something of the Kabbalah as a philosopher today would be expected to know something of Zen. On the other hand, Swedenborg was nothing if not a mystic and a visionary, and as his biographer Martin Lamm points out, "The history of mysticism teaches us that it is neither by their reading nor through personal influences that the great mystics generally realize their mission. On a closer look, one finds that the beginning of their mystical commitment is more often related to a personal experience that they considered to be divine revelation." Swedenborg certainly regarded his understanding of the internal sense of the Word as being revealed by the Lord. He did not think it had arisen out of his study of Philo or of Hermetic and Kabbalistic literature. On this point, I suggest, we must take him at his word.

A Life in Two Worlds

IN THE YEARS BETWEEN 1749 AND 1756, Swedenborg lived in obscurity, writing *Secrets of Heaven*, which was published in London in eight quarto volumes, one volume coming out more or less each year. During this time, he settled into the life that he would lead for the remainder of his days. For his first years on his Stockholm property, which covered about an acre, he lived in a small country house he shared with the gardener, the gardener's wife, and their three daughters. In 1752, he constructed a garden house for his own use. A simple and austere building, it contained a parlor, a bedroom, an orangerie or conservatory, and a study in which Swedenborg did his writing. In later years, Swedenborg's friend Robsahm would observe that the house "was no doubt comfortable for him, but not for anyone else." The bedroom was never heated; Swedenborg slept under three or four English woolen blankets when it was cold. He kept no books here except his Hebrew and Greek Bibles and the indices to them that he had prepared. The study also contained a small stove on which he brewed his coffee, which he drank, heavily sugared, in large amounts throughout the day. Both the orangerie and the garden contained a wide range of plants, many of them exotic to Sweden. Swedenborg's records indicate that he planted chamomile, artichokes, and lemons, and that he ordered a variety of rare seeds and plants from the New World, including corn, watermelon, mulberries, dogwood, and beech.

As Swedenborg advanced into old age, the physical world seemed to recede from him, and he lived half among humans, half among spirits. Sometimes he spoke aloud when conversing with spirits, but usually the conversations were conducted in silence. It is clear from his descriptions of these encounters that they took place in the realm of the mind—that is, he did not hear them with his physical ears or see them with his physical eyes. In fact he insists that this is impossible: "We cannot possibly see [heavenly sights] with our physical eyes, but as soon as the Lord opens our inner eyes—the eyes of our spirit—similar sights can immediately present themselves to view."

These experiences may be best understood by recalling that Swedenborg viewed his journey as an inward one: it was not merely a matter of ascent to the heavens, but of moving deeper within his own being. Thus, he might well have perceived common impulses, emotions, and sensations as external to himself rather than identifying with them, as people ordinarily do. And as the anecdotes above suggest, at this deep inner level one's feelings and attitudes toward something—such as food—are even more tightly interwoven with sensory experience than usual.

THE EIGHTH AND FINAL VOLUME of *Secrets of Heaven* appeared in 1756. It takes Swedenborg's scriptural commentary to the end of Exodus. Although there is some evidence that he intended to offer a spiritual commentary on the whole Bible, he never undertook this effort; the only biblical book that would merit this close attention afterward was the Revelation of John. In 1758, Swedenborg again appeared in London with manuscripts to publish including *Heaven and Hell,* a meticulous account of the many dimensions of the afterlife, which would become Swedenborg's most popular work. It presents a succinct digest of many of the key elements of Swedenborg's theology, including his teaching that heaven has the structure of a human being (the maximus homo or universal human); the doctrine of heavenly marriage, "the union of two people into one mind" that may occur in the afterlife; and the idea that the earth is a proving ground for the human soul, which after death gravitates strictly toward whatever its ruling passion (a concept sometimes translated "love" or "dominant love") was in life and, thus, tends toward heaven or toward hell, after an interval in the intermediate world of spirits.

It is this idea that we move of our own accord toward heaven or hell that represents a key advance in Swedenborg's teaching, for, unlike conventional Christianity, he stresses that heaven is not a reward, nor is hell a punishment. Rather each place is a suitable home for those disposed toward it. In ancient Egyptian art the trial of the soul after death is frequently represented as a weighing of the heart in the scales of good and evil by the gods. Swedenborg's view is similar, except that it is the human heart itself that delivers the verdict. Another comparable perspective appears in *The Tibetan Book of the Dead,* in which the soul in the bardo or intermediate realm is led by its desire to choose its next incarnation. Swedenborg's doctrine differs from traditional Buddhist thought, however, inasmuch as it holds that we can only pass through life once. He rejects reincarnation, an idea known in the West since at least the time of Plato.

In Swedenborg's *Last Judgment,* the earth is not dissolved or the moon turned to blood; the event takes place in dimensions unseen to the physical eye. But Swedenborg says he was permitted to see this event with his spiritual vision. "I was allowed to see all these things with my own eyes so that I could testify to them. This *Last Judgment* started in early 1757 and was completed by the end of that year."

This *Last Judgment* does not affect the physical world (which remains largely unchanged), nor did it radically change Swedenborg's life, at least in the short term. On the other hand, he saw his own mission very much in the light of this process. This housecleaning in the spirit world made it possible for human beings on earth to see spiritual truths more directly and more "inwardly." It also created the possibility of a new humankind that would accept and incorporate these insights. Swedenborg saw it as his mission to promulgate them.

SWEDENBORG DID NOT NEGLECT his more conventional duties. At this time Sweden was in a financial crisis brought about by the war with Prussia, in which Sweden had yet again fared badly. The nation's leaders had adopted a familiar yet ruinous means of dealing with this problem: issuing a virtually worthless paper currency. Swedenborg wrote a lengthy paper on the matter, which was presented to the Swedish Diet in November 1760. He argued against the current fiscal policy and incidentally proposed state regulation of the sale of liquor, which he believed had brought great harm in Sweden. The next year he delivered an address defending Sweden's limited monarchy against absolutism. He did not read these addresses himself but simply presented them as reports. A slight stutter, to which he had been prone all his life, made him shy of public speaking.

In these matters, Swedenborg demonstrated his wisdom and clearsightedness, proving that his encounters with the invisible worlds had not unhinged him mentally. What is perhaps most striking about his political statements is that he makes his arguments in purely conventional terms—the only kind his colleagues would have understood and appreciated. Had he inserted claims of religious authority into these papers, he would have undermined his position, and he clearly knew this.

As Swedenborg became more renowned for his visions and teachings about the spirit world, people naturally became curious about him. It is from this era that we have the most vivid descriptions of Swedenborg personally. He was a man of medium height, with clear blue eyes. In demeanor he was polite and good-humored and reluctant to speak about his mystical experiences unless he was directly asked or he believed the person was genuinely interested.

Swedenborg spent much time alone, communing with the spirits and writing, but he generally accepted dinner invitations when they were offered and was regarded as pleasant and urbane company. At home he ate and drank very little apart from enormous quantities of coffee; a roll soaked in milk was his principal meal. But when he dined out as a guest, he would eat what was served and was not averse to drinking wine, which, like his coffee, he preferred heavily sugared. Despite the peculiarities of his diet, he generally enjoyed excellent health throughout his life and attributed the minor ailments he had to attacks from evil spirits. He kept to his own schedule, sleeping and waking as he liked regardless of the hour. He did not require his servants to adjust to the eccentricities of his timetable; consequently, they found that he required almost no attention at all. During his travels abroad, he kept as much as possible to the same manner of life.

WHEN AT HOME IN STOCKHOLM, Swedenborg, normally reclusive, began to receive visitors: clergymen interested in his teachings, nobles wanting him to communicate with dead relatives, even children. A neighbor's daughter asked him on several occasions to show her an angel, and Swedenborg finally yielded to her request: he led her to a curtain, which he pulled aside to reveal the little girl's own image reflected in a mirror.

Another visitor, an Englishman named Green, came bearing a letter from one Immanuel Kant asking for Swedenborg's views on the nature of reality. Swedenborg did not reply directly to Kant. This was perhaps a tactical mistake, because Kant would publish a book in 1766 titled *Dreams of a Spirit Seer,* mocking and deriding Swedenborg and permanently damaging his reputation in learned circles. But Swedenborg had told Green that he was about to publish a book that would answer Kant's questions. The work he had in mind was probably *Divine Love and Wisdom,* published in 1763 (although some say it is the small treatise *Soul–Body Interaction,* which appeared in 1769).

And yet the message of *Divine Love and Wisdom* suggests that Kant's objections were not merely due to an imagined slight or even to Swedenborg's claims of mystical knowledge. The essence of Swedenborg's teaching is strikingly different from Kant's. Kant stressed the ultimate unknowability of reality in itself. He contended that we experience the world only through categories of experience such as time, space, and causality, and that these are essentially impenetrable; human understanding cannot go past them.

For Swedenborg, reality is ultimately knowable; it is the result of "a constant inflow from the spiritual world into the earthly world." Knowledge of any kind is made possible only by an emanation of power from the Lord, and although the human orientation toward the material world ordinarily blocks our understanding of higher realities, there is nothing that intrinsically prevents us from elevating ourselves to those levels. We are impeded not so much by the limits of our minds as by the limits we place on love: "The reason we do not become rational to the highest degree we are capable of is that our love, which is a matter of our intent, cannot be raised up in the same way as our wisdom, which is a matter of our discernment. The love that is a matter of intent is raised only by abstaining from evils as sins and then by those good actions of thoughtfulness that are acts of service, acts that we are then performing from the Lord." Although these ideas may sound unusual, they resonate with an ancient teaching that true wisdom cannot be isolated as a mere intellectual phenomenon. The wise individual must also be a good individual.

Assessment

THE STORY OF SWEDENBORG'S INFLUENCE extends beyond the limits of this essay. Although at one point he estimated that he could count some fifty people who accepted his teachings, soon his followers would assemble themselves into a new denomination. His legacy extends much further than the New Church, of course, and can be seen in the work of such seminal figures as William Blake (1757–1827), Honoré de Balzac (1799–1850), and Charles Baudelaire (1821–1867). To take only one example, the entire Symbolist movement in nineteenth-century art was inspired by Baudelaire's sonnet "Correspondences"—a poem that was in turn inspired by Swedenborg's teachings.

Swedenborg's most profound legacy is perhaps one that remains largely untapped. More than most, his life has an architectonic structure to it. On the one hand, it encompasses an ascent from an investigation of the mineral kingdom to one of the plant and animal realms. When Swedenborg began the age-old quest for the link between the soul and the body, he had to go past reason and rise into the unseen dimensions of the spirit. On the other hand, Swedenborg's journey was also one toward the interior of the self and of the universe. He started at the outward surface of things—with minerals and technology—and went inward to explore human anatomy before reaching the inmost essence of things, which is spiritual and invisible.

RICHARD SMOLEY is the author of several books, including *Forbidden Faith: The Gnostic Legacy from the Gospels to The Da Vinci Code; Inner Christianity: Hidden Wisdom: A Guide to the Western Inner Traditions* (with Jay Kinney), and *The Essential Nostradamus.* He is the former editor of *Gnosis* magazine and is currently editor of *Quest Books.* This essay is a summary of Mr. Smoley's introduction to *Scribe of Heaven: Swedenborg's Life, Work, and Impact* (by Jonathan Rose, et al., eds., published by the Swedenborg Foundation Publishers in 2005).

Mr. Blake Sings

William Blake. *Milton, a Poem* (title page). White line etching/engraving, painted and hand colored, 1804. The Huntington Library, San Marino, California.

WHEN THE EXPECTED WORD ARRIVED, we met in the Strand, as we had done on earlier occasions, thence to the modest Fountain Court residence where, as we knew, we should receive a welcome, unfailing, rich beyond the humble surroundings Mrs. Blake so warmly offered.

Today our mood was different, both of us reluctant, our eyes downcast, and our speech subdued. Little more than a handful of

146

words passed between us. So, each man wrapped in his own thought, made his way through the business of London.

Neither man said it, but we knew that this must be the last sight we should have of Mr. Blake. We had learned that his time now was a question not of days but hours.

Outside the building we found no decorous silence of respect or mourning. In the street the children were at their usual play; it was as though the man and woman within had made known their wish that it might be so. And as we came to the door, a swoop of swallows was about our heads, rushing, irreverent.

The customary quiet after the door had closed behind us seemed to partake of a different quality. Now it struck us as a dead calm.

Had the spirit of the place already departed? No sound reached us from the rooms above, no sound of industry, of busy engraving tool on metal plate. Not even the rustle of paper.

WE HAD NOT LONG TO WAIT, however, before Mrs. Blake descended, thanking us for coming, as though just another visit. Her calm bearing set an example for the hours ahead. After a few words she led us up to the doors of the two rooms that were their whole residence.

We entered the front room where his drawings and frescoes were all about us. This rear chamber oversaw the river and, a few yards behind, the roaring Strand. Despite ourselves our hearts were lifted. Everywhere his prints hung still on cord lines and walls of this workshop home: the large sheets of his vision, bright as lilies of the field, the fruits and blossoms of his unremitting labours.

There was a hushed conversation with Mrs. Blake. She explained, before we entered where he lay, that her husband was quite at peace, experiencing no discomfort, no pain. Indeed, she seemed more intent upon reassuring us than on any anxiety of her own that she herself must have been undergoing. So we found him on his bed, unmoving, his eyes closed, face serene.

And now she was at his side again, Kate, more than excellent cook, more than cheerful, she shared with him in other things—of belief, of shared visions, nurturing visions of her own. Ever his companion, she had been his helpmate in making his plates: taking the impressions off the copper, tinting them. Together they made the sheets and books, and the writing, the designing, printing, and engraving. Truly, this humble pair of chambers, with their sensation of freedom, their aspect towards the Surrey shore, made of this place, as his biographer has said, the threshold of princes . . . .

Here he lay, so motionless that we stood still ourselves for what must have been long minutes, affected by what was to us a noble sight. Bed and man formed the compelling centre of this scene, the stronger for the completeness of the surrounding whole. Everything spoke of provision for a settled life together. With its cooking fire and table, it was both kitchen and dining room, and the corner bed was for sleep. The other, windowed corner held the room's second table where the artist had engraved his designs, his face towards that window that lent him light to labour and, between the depths of houses, showed a peep of Thames and Thames mud, of Surrey's hills and Kent beyond. On the table we saw the same tools lying ready as if waiting only for the maker's return to his daily duties.

HE HAD BEEN STRONG THROUGH THESE LAST DAYS, even until this present. He had sent out for fresh pencils with one of his last shillings. Despite any decline of his powers, he had worked on his *Europe, The Ancient of Days*, a commission from the younger Tatham, and he had completed it to his satisfaction.

To the last hours, one might see in him still the boy that wandered London's fields or worked with such intent among the great models he was set to copy in Westminster Abbey. Proud to be a Son of Labour yet he was, too, a faithful Son of Liberty, and no mere talker, neither: his personal warning it was that had saved Paine's life.

Nor had these majestic, grand perceptions been lightly won. His was no aloof existence of tranquil vision, but one that was real and passionate. Friends knew how he had endured and anguished in his life. They were acquainted with the ordeals he had been subjected to: that Quarter Sessions torment of Chichester and the Disgraced Sergeant Scholfield; the wrestling with his destiny—the pen his terror, the pencil his shame . . .

*O why was I born with a different face?
Why was I not born like the rest of my race?*

Those who have talked more casually of his "insane genius" were surely less familiar than others who witnessed plain sanity with which he would pronounce, "I am Socrates." Or Moses, or the prophet Isaiah. Such things were natural, part and parcel of that world of ideas he inhabited. And Kate, too, ever an angel to him, as now—how often she had sat thus with her husband. Those domestic images of Job and wife, exactly so. . . .

From time to time noises reached us from without—of Strand or London, or closer at hand, the sound of wheels or children at play.

We had made to leave, but Mrs Blake encouraged us to stay. So it was we passed those last hours with them. Yet it was no brooding, melancholy time. Blake was welcoming—still the host, wakeful for much of this period, even alert and aware of our presence.

For ourselves, though by dusk half-drowsing, we too entered a visionary suspension of reality. We became caught up in a reverie, part of our own thought and reflection, part, also, woven of the words he spoke now, as well as words of his we recollected from past occasions. None of this latter was surprising, seeing how many of his images encircled us on wall, on table. We were in the midst of a world, a universe of his making: Job, Flea and Tyger were the pictures of our minds.

He who beheld whole Worlds in grains of sand, discovered Heavens in the wild flower—he who had instructed us how humankind was made for joy and woe together, had lived his days continually in Eternity's sunrise, being in himself Imagination entire.

While the lilywhite shall in love delight,
Nor a thorn, nor a threat, stain her beauty bright—

Though his eyes were often open in the passage of these hours, we supposed them to be fastened on larger sights than ourselves or his near surroundings. But it came to us that so much of the man remained that he was as we had always known him: expression of the face, the stillness of contemplation, the particular character of his nose, even its small, clenched nostril.

Despite the cheerful air of the couple, we could not but feel some sense of distress that was something more than mere melancholy or self-pity at the prospect of losing such a master and friend. He seemed to divine our emotions or events surrounding himself in the room. Whatever the cause his words now came as if directed at us:

Man was made for joy and woe;
And when this we rightly know,
Thro' the world we safely go—

Though familiar to us from those lips, they seemed to have new meaning. Verses had always emanated from him as naturally and unforced as the tree puts forth its leaves.

There followed hours of silence broken at intervals by Blake's voice. Once, as we thought he had forgotten our presence, he opened his eyes, direct and bold he turned his face toward us, earnestly, as if to reassure us, and said: "Friends, you will know of me how I am in God's presence night and day, and he never turns his face away. . . ."

IN THE LAST OF THE DAY, both man and wife seemed to unite in bringing us into a state that is something more than mere acceptance. What we witnessed is proof of the life as he has lived it—of his fiery conviction that all is come from the spiritual world for good and not for evil. Perhaps we should have felt some shame to have expected anything different, but we did not. Blake put any such thought to flight straightaway, and not by the warmth of his recognition alone, but with his talk. The body of the man undoubtedly was weak, yet the old interest still flourished here, the divine spark that had continually informed his discourse. And this animation was the more commanding now since it was necessarily punctuated by periods of rest and stillness in these hours.

More than once, it seemed such respite had only been to regather his forces in order to break forth once more in fresh utterance. Until these intervals increased their length and he lapsed into a silence of such duration that we could not but suppose it to be the last of all. Scarcely he breathed. Both life and death mingled with the divine future he had always looked to with such expectation. This happy fusion was surely no more than he had known and practiced.

After a little we quit the chamber for the couple to be alone together. All was quiet, within, without, as we waited, glad in our patience, in the tranquillity of that still place. That still air.

When Mrs. Blake came out again to invite us to make what must be our last farewells, we offered our fumbling words of consolation. Now she lifted her frank and open face to us and told us how, with the utmost affection, he had assured her that he should always be about her—would be ever present to take care of her.

There was no word spoken by any of us. We attended him in a silence which endured long enough for us to believe it marked the final decline. No word, no motion from him.

But we had reckoned without the swallows. For then:

"See them!"

It was not us but the man on the bed who caught the last twilight flash past the window.

"See them!" he urged again. "So they come each year in season, as messengers to us."

Perhaps Mrs. Blake was the only one in the room to remain unsurprised. His own bold cry gave way to silence, and we supposed the effort to have taxed his remaining powers. Those were his words. His eyes closed once more.

For our part, we sat rapt in contemplation: this fleeting incident appeared wonderful to us—not least as we considered how the ailing man could have apprehended the mad dash of a whirlwind second, too fast for one in his condition to take in.

In my own mind there arose memory of other, past happenings as when the artist had been at Shoreham with Palmer, and Blake alone mysteriously had sensed a friend's approach, all unexpected, while he was yet a mile and more distant from the house, and not, as they all supposed, well on his road to London. And had he sensed his swallows thus?

Now this was not the end of our astonishment. Yet again he broke upon our reverie, and—Mr Blake began to sing! His wife stood so serenely by, and he sang his love for her:

> *Love to faults is always blind;*
> *Always is to joy inclin'd—*

Not for the first or last time in these hours were we made calm by his conduct. By hers also, as she, yet at his side, joined hands with him. His voice thin, yet clear, he sang of his London also:

> *—The fields from Islington to Marybone*
> *To Primrose Hill and Saint John's Wood—*

Sang his Vision of the City:

> *builded over with pillars of gold;*
> *And there Jerusalem's pillars stood*

Sang of London's People:

> *—The hum of multitudes was there,*
> *but multitudes of lambs—*

Yes, not least he hymned her innocent, poor children:

> *—Thousands of little boys and girls*
> *raising their innocent hands. . .*

Cheerily he sang of youth – yes, lustily:

> *—Let age and sickness rob*
> *The vineyards in the night;*
> *But those who burn with vigorous youth*
> *Pluck fruits before the light—!*

He sang of his high art, all of it executed within confines of their retreat:

> *all of it true to his fierce assertion how:*
> *Great things are done when men and mountains meet;*
> *This is not done by jostling in the street*

No more than a hint of shadow in the fading light, swallows passed the window, gathering for long flight.

A while later he opened his eyes for the last time, and, not singing, but speaking, he said:

> *Sweet Mercy leads me on*
> *With soft repentant moan:*
> *I see the break of day . . .*

And, truly, we believed him!

When we left, this emotion, more of rejoicing than any dejection, persisted in us, filling minds and spirits. Chins raised, eyes uplifted, we trod with firm step. As we made our way, once more we heard that voice, those thoughts as of a prophet, clear as ever.

In our mind's eye we saw, too, those rich images—of Flea and Tyger, of Job, of the Almighty, of the human form divine—representations that daily visited him, that divinely entered the great imagination of this unique man.

So, some of the sadness we had earlier felt was now relieved. Or, rather, mixed with other emotions, not least, of hope, of resolution—of a courage renewed even.

We went from there, back into the world of men as giants refreshed. We left behind the tranquil backwater of our good friend, yet still it marched with us, and our steps were light. We marched, and before long, with no evident signal to each other, we broke into song—there, in the public street—to the astonishment of bystanders and passers-by, repeating those lines the master had given us. Yes. Yes—lustily!

> —*Rouse—Rouse up, Rouse up,*
> *O Young Men—Young Men*
> *Of this New Age—!*

Postscript

On the following Friday of that August, Mr. Blake was interred at the Bunhill Fields burying ground in Finsbury. Calvert, Richmond, Tatham, and others were in that party which accompanied him on that last earthly journey. With the city's traffic noise around, here was company worthy of such a giant. Good dissenting fellowship. For close at hand lay Bunyan, Defoe, and other fellowship.

So we left him there.

TONY WEEKS-PEARSON has written a number of novels during and after twenty years of teaching high-school English. "Mr. Blake Sings" is from the author's recent short-story collection; the debt to Gilchrist's classic biography is evident. The author suggests that his best claim to fame may be as witness to Swedenborgian minister George Dole's performance as sole American competitor in the first Four-Minute Mile, Oxford, England, 1954.

CAROL LEM

Shooting Star

Not until moving to this canyon
had I seen a star shooting out

of a black milky December sky
like a silver arrow,
catching the corner of my eye
as the glass touched my lips.

I sipped thinking of nothing
in particular but now this piercing hit
at the center of the target,
the thought it could all disappear:

that moon the other night
rising behind the mountain ridge
like the first light of creation,

the oak trees, cacti, bougainvillea,
climbing bamboo, and names
I'll never know easing my weariness
of a long day
as much as this petite syrah—
all gone.

And through the French doors
of this balcony observation post,
the books with their marginalia
so carefully penned for that return visit
that never comes
call from the inner rooms

like a parent, "It's getting late,
you better come in now."

But the stubborn child wants her
twinkling stars too
while they're still here
and those words that drop by
like unexpected friends
you invite in to drink with you.

For we still have this evening
and the mountain air as crisp as a page
of a freshly opened book.

So let us sit back and look up.
Whatever falls from the sky
will not go wasted.

Since moving to the tranquil canyon of Sierra Madre, CAROL LEM has become aware of stars, deer, cicadas, and oak trees. A nightly routine, which she calls her zazen or sitting meditation, is watching where her mind goes while observing the sights, sounds, and smells from her balcony. Carol, who teaches creative writing and literature at East Los Angeles College, has recently published a memoir essay with poems in the *Embracing Relationships* issue of the Chrysalis Reader, as well as poems in *Rattle, Open Windows,* and *The Tebot Anthology of California Poets*. A reading of her poems from *Shadow of the Plum,* accompanied by a Japanese bamboo flute, may be heard on her CD, *Shadow of the Bamboo.*

Recliner

IT CAME OVER LEON ONE AFTERNOON that he ought to buy a chair, something new to sit in while he read and took notes. He already had one, a serviceable chair made of oak with a red corduroy seat. But Leon had recently retired from teaching and was enamored with the idea of finding something new in which to sit out the later years of his bookish life. After consulting with his wife, it was resolved that the old chair would go to the basement until it ended up with his daughter in Vermont. She was the collector in the family. She had a barn.

Leon set out the next morning to search for something new. He went alone, having told his wife he'd been looking forward to a leisurely prowl through the various stores and shops. At first she resisted, fearing that, without her, he was sure to return with something that did not fit the general scheme of things. What saved him from her supervision was that the chair would reside in Leon's study, a room truly his and not, therefore, subject to her decorator's eye.

His first stop was a place that seemed to feature recliners. "Is there anything I can show you?" asked a young woman in a blazer and plaid skirt. Overwhelmed by the odor of fresh upholstery, Leon did not actually hear her. Vertigo set in as he scanned the vast floor of loungers. Lines of them rolled away like ocean waves. He reeled, trying to locate himself and then fixed his eye on a leather model behind which a man of glossy cardboard stood, pointing to the chair.

"Who's that?" he inquired.

"Who's who?" she replied.

"The man behind the chair." He pointed to a life-size mockup.

"Oh . . . him?" By now, Leon had regained his bearings and was amused that she didn't know. Neither did he, but then he'd left his glasses in the car. She called to a young man in a white shirt and tie standing far away. "Jerry…" He squinted in their direction. "Who's this cardboard guy that you put behind the black Swivel-Glide?"

"What?"

"The cardboard guy. Who is he?"

"Perry Como . . . I think," he said.

Leon moved closer. The saleswoman followed. "No, this isn't Perry Como," he said.

"It isn't?"

"Absolutely not."

She was growing impatient. "Well, is there something else? Perhaps a chair I could show you?" She gestured with a graceful wave.

"Yes . . . a chair," he said, still fixed on the cardboard man endorsing the black Swivel-Glide. "You know, I don't know who this is either, but it isn't Perry Como, that's for sure."

"Doesn't matter," she said. "Want to try it out?"

"This one?" Leon asked. She'd taken him by surprise. Until then, he'd never even considered such a chair.

"It's our top-of-the-line lounger," she began. "It's real leather but treated so that all you have to do is wipe it with a moist cloth no matter what gets spilled on it." Leon considered the chair, tried to imagine it in his little room. He knew his wife would object at first.

"I wasn't really thinking of one like this."

"Go ahead," she said softly. Something in her manner, perhaps the way she encouraged him, caused Leon to think of his daughter.

"I didn't get your name," he said gently.

"Jill," she replied, putting a finger to the tag pinned on the lapel of her blazer.

"Of course . . . Jill . . ." He smiled and settled into the sumptuous lounger. "Oh my . . . this is elegant, isn't it?"

"Now just reach down there . . . on your right . . ."

Leon found the handle she was referring to, pulled it back, and watched his feet come up. Sudden embarrassment overtook him as he realized how scuffed the toes of his shoes were. Shopping for a lounger requires a shine, he observed as the back and seat began to vibrate. "This switch controls the massage," she said, holding a small control box. She offered it to him. "Just dial the amount you want." Leon took it with nervous interest but did not alter the setting.

"I imagine this could be quite relaxing."

"Depends on the customer," she said. "Some people prefer the basic chair. It can save you about two hundred dollars if you buy the chair without it. But either way you're getting a lot of chair." Leon passed the control box back to her. She turned it off.

"Either way . . ." he repeated. Behind him, he could feel the flat man looming. Just who was he? It vexed Leon that he didn't know, that nobody seemed to know. He let his feet down and got up. "A very nice chair, but the problem is I tend to work at my desk. I guess, in the back of my mind, I was looking for a chair I could use at my desk."

"Ah . . ." she said. "I'm sorry to say we only stock loungers. That's what we're about . . . loungers . . . recliners."

"So I see." Leon surveyed the floor as if to confirm it.

"I wonder if an office-supply store would be more what you're looking for." She spoke helpfully, but to his surprise Leon found that he did not like the sound of that. Maybe it wasn't a new chair that he wanted after all. Maybe it was a second chair that he'd come looking for, a second one that, unconsciously, he'd been wanting all along?

"What's the price of this leather one minus the vibrating feature?" he asked.

"Let's see . . ." she said mirroring his reversal perfectly. "Minus the massage it's . . . I'll have to check to be sure." She went over to the desk where she consulted a notebook and then came back with it open, studying the figures as she did. "The Swivel-Glide in black, no massage . . . thirteen-ninety-nine . . . but I can let it go for . . . nine-ninety-nine. So you're saving four hundred dollars."

"And you have one in stock?"

"The book says we've got four, two without the massage, two with."

"I do like it," he said. She made no reply, preferring to let silence force the moment. "You've got a deal," he said. "But only if you throw the display in with it."

"The display?"

"Him," Leon said, pointing to the cardboard man smiling beside the recliner.

"You want Perry Como thrown in?"

"That isn't Perry Como," Leon reminded her.

"Well, whoever it is . . ." she said, struggling to preserve her *sangfroid*. "If you'll excuse me, I'll have to run this by Jerry." Leon nodded and watched her go. Jerry lowered his head and listened. When she came back smiling, Leon knew they had a deal.

LEON'S WIFE WAS WORKING IN A FLOWER BED when he pulled into the driveway. When she heard the mini-van's door close, she planted her trowel in the earth and turned to wave. There was her husband walking toward the house with a life-size silhouette tucked under his arm.

"Leon!"

"Yes dear?"

"What are you doing?"

"Going into the house?"

"I mean with that . . . thing." She moved quickly. "What is it, for heaven's sake?"

"*Who* is the question," he said and kept going.

The side facing her was nothing but blank cardboard. She went around to see what he might be getting at. "Did you find a chair?"

"Sure did. A real beauty," he told her.

She was torn between holding back the cardboard man who was about to enter her home and going over to the van to see what her husband had bought.

"I didn't expect you to find something so quickly," she said.

"Neither did I, but I fell in love with the first one I tried."

"Sounds like us," she quipped. Leon would have smiled, but he was positioning himself just then to angle the man in head first. "Would you hold the screen, Dear?"

"Where do you think you're going with that?"

"My room," he said confidently.

"For how long?" she inquired.

"I don't know . . . until I figure out who he is, I guess."

"I hope you do, Leon. We can't have that thing in the house."

"Then I'll put it the garage."

"We can't have it in the garage, either."

"Why not?"

"People will see it when the door goes up."

"So what?"

"Leon!" She followed him down the hall to his study where he dragged the cardboard man to a far corner and set him up. "I want you to keep the door to this room closed until you're finished with him. Is that clear, Leon?"

"Does he bother you that much?"

"He'd . . . bother anyone . . . with that smile and . . . cheap suit."

"Come on, Rose. I admit the suit's a little shiny, but he's got a pleasant face." She considered his observation. It was always like this. After the initial shock, she'd catch a little of Leon's fire and grow interested herself.

"He does look familiar, doesn't he?" she said.

"The kids at the furniture store didn't know who he was either. One of them thought he was Perry Como!"

"No!"

"And then the other one, the young lady who actually sold me the chair? I don't think she even knows who Perry Como was."

"Well . . ." Rose considered it in her usual, balanced way. "How old was she?"

"About the same age as Elizabeth."

"I guess that's no surprise then."

Opposite:
Baby in Red Chair.
Oil on canvas,
ca. 1810–1830.
Abby Aldrich Rockefeller
Folk Art Museum,
The Colonial
Williamsburg Foundation,
Williamsburg, Virginia.

"No surprise? When you and I were in our twenties, we certainly knew our parents' music. We knew about Glen Miller and Frank Sinatra and . . ."

"Times have changed, Dear," she said evenly.

"They certainly have," he agreed. "And that's why I had to get out of it. Kids today are no longer educable, not in the way . . ."

"Leon," she said, interrupting his favorite diatribe. "Aren't we going to see your new chair?"

"The chair! I forgot all about it. Is Ralph home?"

"Yes, I just finished talking with him and Loraine."

"Good, I'll call him right up."

"His back's out again."

"Then maybe you and I can get it in," Leon suggested.

"I don't see why not," she said. "It's not that heavy, is it?"

"No. In fact it's the lighter of the two models because I got it without the vibrator. You know, a sort of massage feature? The cardboard man was standing right behind it," he added proudly.

"I see . . ."

Leon opened the van's sliding door. "So how do you like it?" Rose blinked thoughtfully. She hadn't expected a handsome recliner.

"It's rather . . . elegant," she replied.

"The very same word I used!" he said, savoring his small triumph.

"Are you going to put the cardboard man behind it? I mean the way he was . . . at the furniture store?" she asked.

"Maybe . . . for a little while. Until I figure out who he is, anyway. And then . . ." Leon began to realize that he didn't actually know what he was going to do with the cardboard man or if he was even willing to share his room with him. "I am curious about him, though . . ." Rose knew instantly what he was thinking.

"Elizabeth and Andy are coming for dinner tonight, maybe they'll know."

"Terrific!" he said. "And they'll get to see my new chair, too." Now he found himself wishing he'd bought the vibrating model, but it was too late for that. "All set?" he asked, leaning into the van.

Rose did not hear him. An image of her daughter's barn was growing clear in her mind. There, in a loft of castaway furniture, stood the cardboard man smiling in his shiny suit. Sunlight warmed the beams as swallows circled above his head. Yes, she thought, in Elizabeth's barn. It was simply a matter of finding out who he was.

VINCENT DECAROLIS lives in Freeport, Maine. He devotes most of his time to writing poetry and fiction. His scholarly interests include, especially, the writings of James Joyce, C.G. Jung, and New Testament studies. "Recliner" marks his fifth contribution to the Chrysalis Reader.

Part I: Wish You Were Here

No one can know what the restful peace of the outer person is like or the restlessness brought on by cravings and falsities, who has not experienced a state of peace. This state is so full of delight that it overflows every concept of delight. It is not just the ending of stuggle but is a life that comes from a more inward peace, moving the outer person in ways beyond description. Then truths of faith and good gifts of love are born that draw their life from the delight of peace.

—EMANUEL SWEDENBORG, *SECRETS OF HEAVEN*, 92

Part II: Breaking Out

The issue in our [deeper] trials is whether the evil will gain control that is in us from hell or the good that is in us from the Lord. The evil that wants control is in the natural or outer person, while the good is in the spiritual or inner person. As a result, even in our trials, the issue is the control of one over the other. If the evil wins, then the natural person controls the spiritual; if the good wins, then the spiritual person controls the natural.

—EMANUEL SWEDENBORG, *SECRETS OF HEAVEN*, 8961

Part III: Sea Changes

[When we are being reborn] our first state is a tranquil one; but as we are making the passage into the new life, we pass also into a state of disturbance. The evil and false things we have absorbed in the past are coming out . . . and disturbing us, eventually with such force that we are caught in trials and harassments by the hellish crew, which is trying to destroy the state of our new life. Still, at the deepest level, we have a state of peace. Unless this were at our deepest level, we would not fight. We are actually focusing on it as our goal throughout the struggles we are involved in, and unless it were our goal, we would not have the energy or the strength to fight.

—EMANUEL SWEDENBORG, *SECRETS OF HEAVEN*, 3696.2

Part IV: The Big Ticket

[Swedenborg takes the six days of creation as symbolic of six successive stages of spiritual growth. The following is his summary, which introduces a verse-by-verse, full-chapter treatment.]

The six days of times, which are six successive states of human rebirth, are in general terms like this.

[continued next page]

These translations (pp. 161–162) are from *A Thoughtful Soul: Reflections from Swedenborg*, edited and translated by George F. Dole. Swedenborg Foundation Publishers, Chrysalis Books, 1995.

The FIRST STATE *is the one that precedes—both the state from infancy and the state just before rebirth. It is called void, emptiness, and darkness. And the first motion, which is the Lord's mercy, is the spirit of God hovering over the face of the water.*

The SECOND STATE *is one in which a distinction is made between the things that are the Lord's and the things that belong to the person. The things that are the Lord's are called "The remnants" in the Word and are primarily insights of faith that have been learned from infancy. These are stored away and do not surface until the person reaches this state, which rarely happens nowadays without trial, misfortune, or depression, which deaden the physical and worldly concerns that are typically human. In this way, the concerns of the outer person are seprated from those of the inner. The remnants are in the inner person, stored away there by the Lord for this time and for this use.*

The THIRD STATE *is one of repentance, in which the individual, from the inner person, does talk reverently and devoutly and does bring forth good [actions] that resemble deeds of compassion. Still, they are not really alive because they are thought to be done independently. They're called the tender plant, the seed-bearing plant, and, finally, the fruit tree.*

The FOURTH STATE *occurs when the individual is moved by love and enlightened by faith. Before this, the person did indeed talk reverently and bring forth good [actions]—but out of a state of trial and constraint, not out of faith and compassion. So now faith and compassion are kindled in the inner person and are called the two great lights.*

The FIFTH STATE *is the one in whch the individual talks from faith, and consequently, strengthens his or her devotion to what is true and good. The things now brought forth are alive and are called the fish of the sea and the birds of the air.*

The SIXTH STATE *occurs when the person says what is true and does what is good from faith, and therefore, from love. The things now brought forth are called the living soul and the animals. And since the individual is then beginning to act from both faith and love, he or she becomes a spiritual person, who is called an image [of God]. The spiritual life of such a person is delighted and nourished by things related to insights of faith and to deeds of compassion, which are called "food," and the natural life is delighted and nourished by things related to the body and the senses. This results in conflicts until love gains control, and the person becomes heavenly.*

Not all people who are being reborn reach this state. Some—most people nowadays—reach only the first; some, only the second. Some reach the third, fourth, and fifth; few, the sixth; and hardly anyone, the seventh.

—EMANUEL SWEDENBORG, *SECRETS OF HEAVEN,* 6–13